50

DON'T SWEAT THE SMALL STUFF FOR MEN

Also by the author:

Don't Sweat the Small Stuff for Women (by Kristine Carlson)
Don't Sweat the Small Stuff for Teens
Don't Sweat the Small Stuff in Love (with Kristine Carlson)
Don't Sweat the Small Stuff at Work
Don't Sweat the Small Stuff with Your Family
Don't Sweat the Small Stuff About Money
Don't Sweat the Small Stuff…and It's All Small Stuff
Slowing Down to the Speed of Life (with Joseph Bailey)
Handbook for the Heart (with Benjamin Shield)
Handbook for the Soul (with Benjamin Shield)
Shortcut Through Therapy
You Can Feel Good Again
You Can Be Happy No Matter What

DON'T SWEAT
THE SMALL STUFF
FOR MEN

Simple Ways to Minimize Stress
in a Competitive World

RICHARD CARLSON, PH.D.

HYPERION
New York

LIBRARY OF CONGRESS CATALOGING-IN-PUBLICATION DATA

Carlson, Richard.
    Don't sweat the small stuff for men : simple ways to minimize stress in a competitive world / by Richard Carlson.—1st ed.
      p. cm
    ISBN 0-7868-8636-6
    1. Conduct of life. 2. Peace of mind. 3. Men—Psychology. I. Title

BF637.C5 C318   2001
158.1'081—dc21   2001024467

FIRST EDITION

10 9 8 7 6 5 4 3 2 1

This book is dedicated to the most important man in my life—
my father and good friend, Don Carlson.
I love you.

ACKNOWLEDGMENTS

I would like to thank and acknowledge the following people for their assistance in the creation of this book. My father, Don Carlson, for being the most important male influence in my life. My dear friend and mentor, Marvin Levin, for the countless hours of counsel and patient advice he has given me over the years. My dear friends Benjamin Shield and Joe Bailey for always being there for me. My assistant, Nicole Walton, for her dedication to making my life easier. And the thousands of men who have written or shared with me over the years. I'd also like to offer a special thanks to my wife, Kristine, for her support and loving presence in my life; my kids, Jazzy and Kenna, for their unconditional love and the incredible joy they bring to my life. I'd also like to thank my editor at Hyperion, Leslie Wells, for her helpful guidance and supportive friendship, and my agents, Patti Breitman and Linda Michaels, for their support and encouragement, both personally and professionally. Finally, I'd like to thank my mother and good friend, Barbara Carlson, for being a special influence throughout my life.

CONTENTS

INTRODUCTION

In a few weeks, I'll celebrate forty years of being a man. Well, actually, a good number of those years I was a boy, but you know what I mean.

For as long as I can remember, I've been interested in what makes people tick and what makes them fall apart (or stress out, as it's often called). I've always been curious as to the reasons why some people are happy, while others seem so troubled; why some people respond to life, taking the minor hassles in stride, while others react so strongly and adversely to the same types of irritations. I've long asked the question, Why are some people grateful for the gift of life, while others seem to take it so much for granted? Over the years, I've developed a few ideas that might explain, to some degree, the answers to these questions.

You might be familiar with some of the *Don't Sweat the Small Stuff* books that I have written. In each book, my goal has been to share simple, commonsense strategies geared toward a particular type of reader. This one was written and tailored just for you—men. Needless to say, we're quite different from our female counterparts!

Those familiar with the so-called "self-help" category are aware that, usually, it's women, not men, who buy and enjoy the majority of the books. However, over the years, I've been amazed by the thousands of men who have written to me to share a story or just to say thanks. The letters, phone calls, e-mails, and personal conversations I've had have taught me a great deal about men: where we are coming from, what we want, what bothers and frustrates us, and perhaps most importantly, which types of suggestions seem to help the most. Although the stories I've received have been very different, one thing has become abundantly clear. Given the opportunity, most men jump at the chance to become less stressed and more happy. I've found that we are more willing to look at life in new ways than we are often given credit for.

While we are obviously all very different from one another, we nevertheless have a great deal in common. When you get to know men you discover that, beneath the surface, we share many of the same fears, worries, and frustrations—but also many of the same joys, hopes, and dreams.

As you well know, being a man isn't always easy. There are all sorts of expectations imposed upon us—some realistic, others not so realistic. I want you to know, up front, that I share many of the same struggles that you do. I approach my personal life, not as an expert, but as a fellow student. While I do pretty well most of the time, there are times when I, like you, stress out. I get angry, frustrated, and worried. What I have learned, however, is to minimize the times that this happens. But when it does happen, I've discovered some pretty effective tricks to get me back on track relatively quickly. I don't for a minute think it's possible to have a perfect life, but I do believe that most of us have the capacity to create more joy and inner peace in our lives.

Men have a number of built-in strengths. Unfortunately, along with those strengths, come a few built-in problem areas. For example, as a rule, we're highly competitive and driven to succeed. Our competitive natures, while helpful in certain areas, can also lead to a degree of stress and burnout.

Men can be pretty stubborn, as well. And while there are certain advantages to being stubborn in terms of achieving a desired result, stubbornness can interfere with nourishing relationships. It can also, without our even knowing it, prevent us from being quick learners and good listeners (the latter being one of the things that drives women nuts about us!). Being stubborn can also encourage us to be a bit defensive and can keep us from seeing the contributions we make to our own problems—a major ingredient in personal growth.

Another thing about us men is that most of us seem to be in a constant hurry. We are often running just a little late, scrambling to our next appointment—personal or professional. And while there is some validity to the "efficiency argument," we can, at times, get going so fast and furious that we miss what's right in front of us. We become so preoccupied with what's next, that we forget to enjoy and experience what's now. By learning to become a bit more present and slightly less rushed, we can bring a great deal more peace and joy to our daily lives and to our relationships.

Obviously, there are other aspects of being a man that have the potential to cause us at least some degree of frustration. The good news is that, when you have an open mind and you're willing to practice a bit, you can improve these difficult areas.

I was asked in front of an audience whether I felt that stress was a motivator. The man asking the question, seemingly stressed himself, was concerned about what might happen to a man's motivation, his "edge" and chances of success, if he were to become "too relaxed." I wouldn't worry too much about that! In other words, while anything is possible, I don't think it's very likely that most of us have to be concerned about becoming too relaxed. Most of us are pretty stressed, with plenty of tension to spare.

My goal is a bit more realistic. I'm going to share with you ways to become slightly more relaxed, ways to take the edge off and to move in the general direction of happier, more peaceful living.

Incidentally, without the ongoing distraction of mental stress and irritation, it's easier to live a more effective and successful life. It's my feeling that small, incremental movements toward less stressed living can make a world of difference in the quality of your life. By becoming a little less reactive, we are able to take more things in stride. By becoming a bit less irritable, we are able to maintain a healthy sense of humor. By heightening our perspective, even a little bit, we are able to keep our priorities straight and see the bigger picture. By embracing kindness and compassion, we are able to enhance our relationships and our connection to the world at large. And by being slightly less stressed and frazzled, we can learn to stop sweating the small stuff.

I hope you have as much fun reading this book as I did writing it. It's not brain surgery, but I honestly feel it can be enormously helpful if you give it a chance. There are a number of advantages to becoming happier and less stressed. I hope you'll give these strategies a fair shot at making your life even better than it already is. Good luck!

1

HAVE AN AFFAIR

I thought the title of this strategy would grab your attention and would be a great place to begin this book.

Okay, not that kind of affair!

The kind of affair I'm talking about is a love affair with life. If there's one thing I've noticed that seems to be lacking in many men, it's a passion for life. It seems that many of us have lost that sense of wonder and awe for the incredible gift of life itself. We've become lost in the multitude of responsibilities, ambitions, drive, and commitments. We've become very serious and heavyhearted. Many of us have lost our sense of humor and our perspective. We've lost our compassion, as well. Instead of marveling at it all, we take life for granted. We become stuck in the mundane and succumb to boredom. It's as if we're doing nothing more than putting in time and going through the motions.

Life is slowly passing us by. Without a genuine sense of enthusiasm, a zest for life and a lighthearted spirit, we take our problems and obstacles too seriously. We become uptight and a drag to be around. More than anything else, we start sweating the small stuff. Life starts to bother us instead of amusing us. People are seen as burdens instead of as gifts. Challenges are dreaded instead of seen as opportunities.

The solution to all of this is to have an affair with life. The idea is to reignite your passion for living, and to see the extraordinary in the ordinary. Remind yourself how precious and how short this adventure really is. I read a great book called *A Parenthesis in Eternity*. What a great way to think about the duration of your life—as a blip on a passing screen. We're here for a moment in time—and then we're gone. Why waste one second on self-pity, frustration, irritation, and all the rest? Our lives are so much more important than that.

It's shocking what happens to the quality of your life when you put it into this perspective. All of a sudden, the things that seemed so big seem small. And the things that seemed so small—and the things we postpone and take for granted—seem so big! We see that, for the most part, we usually prioritize in reverse order. But we can change all that in a moment. We can make a shift right now.

The things that we so often attach importance to are important, but it's a question of degree. Success, perfection, achievement, money, recognition—you can have them all, but they're not everything. In fact, without a passion and appreciation for life, they don't amount to much.

I was talking to a group of men about this subject. A few days later, I received a call from one of them that sums up the essence of this strategy. He said that while we were talking, he had thought that my "intentions" were good, but that I didn't really understand how serious and important his "role" was to everyone.

As fate would have it, while driving home that evening, his life changed in a single moment. He was nearly clipped by a huge truck on the freeway. He wasn't hurt, but it was a very close call. The near miss brought forth the insight that he hadn't spent virtually any time with any of his three children in several years, and that they were growing up very quickly. For the first time in years, tears came down his face as he realized that he was missing the point of life—as well as his chance to live it. When he arrived at home, he sat down with his family and told them that he was going to be making some changes in his life, beginning with appreciating his family. He had had a major change of heart.

Although this type of realization often has to do with family, it's not just about family. It's even larger than that. Recognizing the miracle of life—and having an affair with it—means that you begin to attach great value to the moments of everyday life. The people you live and work with—and, for that matter, go grocery shopping with—all take on far more importance. Nature appears more beautiful, life is more precious, conveniences are more appreciated. You become, not less effective, but less demanding on others and on yourself, because you better understand the relative importance and significance of the events around you. Things won't get to you so much, and you won't be sweating the small stuff—at least, not as often!

An affair with life is real, and it can happen to anyone at any time. All it takes is the commitment to reflect upon the miracle of life itself and to remember, each day, how lucky we are to be alive. Think about what it means to wake up in the morning and have another day to live. Someday, that won't be the case. In the meantime, live each day like it really matters—because it does.

One final note on this subject. Needless to say, an affair with life will never get you into any trouble with your wife or girlfriend. On the contrary, they will appreciate your change of heart as much as you do. So have fun.

2

MAKE THE

"PEACEFUL ASSUMPTION"

I'd like to share something with you that, many years ago, changed the way I looked at life. It opened many doors for me in terms of becoming a more peaceful, nonreactive, and effective person. I think you'll see that it's a starting point of sorts. In other words, once you make the peaceful assumption, everything else has a chance to fall into place.

The peaceful assumption says: If not for the fact that I was caught up in something or in a low mood, I'd be feeling peaceful right now. It's a statement reminding yourself that you're aware of the power of your own thoughts to take you away from a peaceful state of mind. The peaceful assumption means you acknowledge the fact that, when you're not feeling peaceful or centered, you're thinking in a way that is contributing to your lack of contentment. You're either thinking negatively or you're too caught up or your mind is filled with thoughts of fear, anger, regret, jealousy, whatever—and you're taking those thoughts very seriously.

Please don't go extreme on me. I'm not suggesting that you're always going to be happy, nor that you should be. Nor am I suggesting that you're going to feel at all peaceful when extremely bad or painful things happen to you. You're not going to be happy if your wife or girlfriend leaves you or has an affair. You're not going to be happy if something happens to your child, you lose your job, your house burns down, or your car is stolen! That's not what the peaceful assumption is all about.

The peaceful assumption is about ordinary, day-to-day, moment-to-moment living. It's like home base, or a starting point. It's a place you live (or at least visit), then drift away from—and come back to.

Since I've made the peaceful assumption in my own life, a typical day will play itself out like this. I usually wake up peaceful (unless I'm in some sort of bad mood). I'll begin my routine, chores, and the business of my day. I may have phone calls to make, a lecture to plan, writing to do, or some plans with the kids.

Invariably, at some point (usually earlier than I'd like), something happens—an unreturned phone call, some bad news, a hassle to take care of—and I start to drift away from my peaceful home base. My thoughts take over, and I start to feel annoyed, bothered, agitated, or stressed.

I become aware that I'm drifting away by the way I'm feeling. Because I've made the peaceful assumption, I know with absolute certainty that I'm contributing to my own feelings of distress. In other words, I know that I'd be feeling peaceful, if not for my own thinking. So now I'm at a fork in the road. I can either continue to think as I am, think harder or more forcefully, or try to analyze what's going on. Or, I can recognize the role my thinking is playing in the way I'm now feeling, and choose to back off for a while. It's totally within my control.

I've found that I'm always more equipped to deal with my life and any problems or hassles that come up when I can keep my bearings and remain calm. Backing off of my thinking allows me to do this. I can then deal more effectively with whatever situation presents itself.

I'd estimate that I come upon dozens of forks in the road virtually every day of my life: plenty of chances to decide whether I will continue on a particular train of thought that will lead me toward sweating the small stuff or, worse, starting to feel stressed and overwhelmed. Or I'll recognize what's happening and back off.

I know it sounds almost too simple, but it's really not. In fact, if you think about it, it's very logical. You have a starting point, you drift away, and then you can either drift back toward "home" or wander even further. Taking this strategy to heart allows for a great deal of personal growth. Making the peaceful assumption means taking absolute responsibility for your own happiness and peace of mind.

3

SPEND MORE TIME WITH
YOUR KIDS

There's no question that more dads than ever before are very involved in their kids' lives. And that's terrific. It's great for the kids,
great for the family unit, great for society, and great for the dads. Everyone
wins.

Many men, however, to a large degree are still missing out on one of
the greatest joys that exists in the world—spending time with their kids,
not out of a sense of responsibility or obligation, but purely by choice. In
other words, we're doing better, but we still have a long way to go.

Whether they are less than a month old or nineteen, kids have incredible gifts to offer us men. The qualities of children complement our
own qualities. In other words, youth, playfulness, lightheartedness, curiosity, and intuition are just what the doctor ordered and usually just what
we need.

Spending time with kids brings a sense of balance to our lives. It
reminds us that the best things in life aren't things. Instead, the magic of
life is revealed by the interactions we have with others, particularly those
we love. In my opinion, kids, more than anyone else, enable us to be
touched by life. I have learned more about life from being a dad than
from anything else.

Years ago someone sent me a cartoon strip that, to this day, is my personal favorite. I haven't seen it in years, and can't remember the cartoonist; however, the message will stick with me forever. The cartoon was a picture of two men entering a large room. A stuffy-looking, formal cocktail party was taking place. The men were all dressed in expensive-looking three-piece suits, and the women were smartly dressed, as well.

The two-word caption read, very simply, "Yipes, grown-ups!"

It hit me like a ton of bricks. It was at the same time both hilarious and meaningful.

Don't get me wrong. There are times I really enjoy, as I'm sure many of you do, a formal get-together, and I have enormous respect for most "grown-ups." However, you must agree that, at times, grown-ups are far too serious! We get caught up in the minutiae of life and focus on all the wrong things. We can be extremely superficial, especially in groups. We get so busy planning for life that we sometimes forget to live.

The more time you spend with kids, however, the less seriously you'll take even the serious adults you spend time with. It seems that you become, to a certain degree, almost immune to any negative effect that might otherwise come your way.

Kids have a great way of telling it the way it is. A few weeks ago, I was, once again, working a bit too hard. My nine-year-old daughter asked me a straightforward question. She said, "Daddy, why don't you just take a few days off?" Not very complicated, is it?

Shortly after our first child was born, I was talking to a man whose youngest son was heading off to college. He said something that others have since repeated. With tears streaming down his face, he said, "If I had to do it over again, my priorities would have been so much different."

I've learned to think of my time with my kids as the gift that it is. I try as hard as I can to prioritize my time and involvement with them, ahead of virtually everything else. At times, it's hard because, as you know, there is always something pressing that needs to be attended to. I've learned, however, that when I go to sleep at night, I never regret a single moment of the time I spend with my kids. I also know that when my kids are grown-ups—only a few more years from now—I'll never regret the time that I spent with them, and I'm sure I'll wish I'd had more.

I can't encourage you enough to spend more time with your kids. And when you do, remind yourself of the gifts they bring to your life. I've never met a man who wasn't happy to have made this decision. I hope you'll make it too.

4

TAKE YOUR WIFE'S ADVICE

In a way, it's ironic: The person who probably knows us as well as anyone in the world is, very often, the person we're least likely to take advice from. That person, of course, is our wife.

There are all sorts of possible explanations. Perhaps we take our wives for granted; we don't take them seriously enough; or we get too defensive. But the fact remains—she really does know us inside and out, including our quirks and weaknesses, and she probably sees at least some of the ways that we get in our own way. And because it's much easier for others to see ways in which we might improve than it is to see those things in ourselves, it can pay enormous dividends if we can muster the humility to pay attention and listen.

A man once told me that he had been laid off, essentially, because he was in the habit of interrupting people; he was a very poor listener. He admitted that his wife had been talking to him about this tendency for years, but that he felt she was nagging him. After the fact, he realized that she had been right all along. Her nagging was simply her attempt to share with him something she was able to see, that he wasn't.

Kris isn't a big-time advice giver, but the advice she has given me has made an enormous difference in my life. Here are a few examples. She suggested that I speak more slowly in public, which I now do—and it has made me a more effective speaker. She suggested that I spend more time alone, which has made me a happier person and a far more reflective thinker. And recently, she suggested that I check with my doctor about a health-related issue. She had a hunch that something might be off. I did, and it turned out that I was in need of some medication. Luckily it wasn't serious, but I've been feeling better ever since.

One day I was complimenting her on how right on she had been on certain things, when she gave me a return compliment. She reminded me that it's always easier to give advice than it is to listen to it. That's sort of the point to this strategy.

I'm not suggesting that our wives' advice is always on target or appropriate, or that there aren't times when they could improve upon their timing and/or delivery. However, it's still the case that in many instances, they do give some great advice.

By listening carefully and taking our wives' advice to heart, there are times that we can either reduce the stress we already have or avoid future stress that is likely to occur. Oh yeah, and one more thing. By taking her advice, you're going to score big points and improve the state of your relationship.

5

AVOID THE "S" WORD

There are certain words—you know what they are—that are prohibited in schools and other places and are considered crude and obnoxious. On a lighter note, I'd like you to consider adding an additional "S" word to your avoidance list. I'm referring here to the word "serious."

Many of us men have become so incredibly serious. We're offended easily and become bothered, irritable, and uptight at the drop of a hat. We walk around with serious looks on our faces as we sweat practically everything. It seems like we're at a point where we take everything too seriously—ourselves, other people, mistakes, plans, hassles, and life in general. We're on edge, almost looking for things to complain about.

One way to combat this tendency is to make light of it. That's why I refer to it as the "S" word. In our home, we remind each other in lighthearted ways when one of us has crossed the line into "serious" territory. One of my daughters, for example, will say, "Dad, you've got that serious look on your face again." There's a way in which keeping a sense of humor about our own seriousness lets us make allowances for the imperfections in life and see that people—all of us—are really characters doing the best we can, flaws and all.

Are there serious aspects to life? Of course there are. Is it appropriate and necessary to feel and act serious some of the time? Absolutely. But that's altogether different from being serious a vast majority of the time. To be too serious, too often, is to miss out on a great deal of the joy of life. I often joke at the end of my talks that very few people on their deathbeds look back on their lives and wish they had been more uptight. To the contrary, you hear lots of touching stories of people looking back over the course of their lives and wondering what all the fuss was about. They realize that many of the things they were so upset and bothered by really weren't such a big deal after all. And, just as importantly, that many of the things they took for granted were the things that really were important.

I don't know about you, but I'm positive that I won't ever be looking back and wishing I had been more uptight.

At some point, we learned to become really serious—so, I believe, we can relearn how to become less serious. Years ago, when I first realized that I was too serious, I wrote the letter "S" in capital letters on a flash card. For about a week, I carried the card around with me in my day planner. Every once in a while, I would glance at it and would be reminded of my goal to take things less seriously. I'd catch myself red-handed acting too uptight.

It actually became funny to me that I would see life as such serious business, but at the same time, I could see my own innocence in the process. Once I adopted a sense of humor about my own serious attitude, it became easier to let it go and take more things in stride. It also became easier to differentiate between small stuff and that which was more significant.

Today, if you were to ask one of my close friends, he or she would tell you that I still take certain things too seriously. But I believe most of them would report that I've made significant progress over the years.

If you can see the value in becoming a little less serious—for yourself and those around you—then you have it in you to do so. Instead of waiting until the end of your life to have a change of heart, make that effort now. You'll be glad you did.

6

DON'T KNOW THE ANSWER

Sometimes I think the three words a man fears most are: I don't know. For whatever reasons, we seem to find security in knowing, or at least thinking that we know, all the answers, possible outcomes, solutions, potential problems, and everything else.

Ironically, however, having to know the answer or always having to know what to do next is quite stressful. It puts constant pressure on us to be on guard; thinking, thinking, always thinking. It keeps us in our heads, encouraging us to imagine the worst. Even when we don't know an answer or what to do next, we come up with something or make something up— so that we appear to know what's going on or look like we're on top of things or "in charge," in order to convince ourselves of the same.

For example, we get ourselves into a mess in our professional lives. We may be overextended or have conflicting agendas. Rather than admit that we are confused, overwhelmed, and don't know what to do, we scramble to come up with an answer, often compounding the very problem we need to solve.

It took me years to realize that, despite outer appearances to the contrary, there is often great peace to be found in not knowing the answer— in not knowing what to do next—and admitting it, to others or at least to oneself. The act of acknowledging that you don't have an answer to a question or that you don't have a solution—at least not yet—seems to clear your mind, release worry, and open the door for your wisdom to surface. The act of clearing your mind—instead of forcing an answer—allows you to see things slightly more clearly, from a fresh perspective. It allows answers to percolate and bubble within you.

I'm not unrealistic. I can easily see how someone—maybe even you—could say, "Yeah, that sounds fine and good, but maybe just a little unrealistic." But step back and think about it for a moment. When you are presented with an issue or a problem, one of two things happens. You either know what to do—and/or what the optimal response is—or you don't. If you do know, it's usually pretty obvious, or it's apparent that you can find out pretty quickly. But if you don't know, what's the point of pretending or forcing an answer?

Recently, I agreed to do something, but then later regretted it. For a while, I struggled. I thought and thought about what to do. My mind explored all the options, and I came up with a number of solutions—all of them bad. My mind was spinning, and I was feeling stressed and consumed.

I discussed the issue with a friend, who pointed out to me that I was trying too hard. It was clear to him that while I wanted to think that I knew what to do, the truth was, I didn't have a clue.

The act of quieting down and letting go of my need to have an immediate answer paved the way for an appropriate solution to come to me. Rather than banging my head against a wall, mentally reviewing the same set of facts, what I really needed to do was to look at it differently. I needed a clear mind, uncontaminated by my existing thoughts on the subject.

The answer came to me the next morning shortly after waking up. In fact, it seemed pretty obvious what to do. I was a little surprised that I hadn't thought of it earlier. The result was that I was able to modify my commitment in such a way that I could accommodate the people involved without feeling overwhelmed.

In retrospect, had I gone with my impulses and my need to know what to do immediately, without reflection, it's clear that I would have ended up exhausted and probably disappointing others.

Being willing to not know involves some degree of faith. You have to be willing to trust that, even though you don't have an immediate answer, you'll be able to come up with an appropriate solution or answer that is ultimately better than any instant reaction.

You can rest assured that there's usually no harm in admitting that you don't know what to do. The fact of the matter is that, in many instances, not knowing may be the best form of knowing. Have faith in yourself. Ultimately, you will know what to do.

7

HAVE A SPECIAL CAUSE

One of the incredible joys I've experienced over the past several years has been receiving tens of thousands of letters from people all over the world. Many of the letters I've received come from people who are sharing ways that they have learned to bring joy and peace into their own lives.

A consistent and encouraging theme from men has been how the introduction of some element of service has brought them tremendous richness and satisfaction. Over and over, men have shared with me that expanding their lives from being solely work- and achievement-driven to the inclusion of service has done wonders for their soul. By incorporating even the slightest amount of work for the good of the world, men are able to bring a sense of balance and even greater meaning to their lives. Everyone seems to agree that, because it takes so little time (and just a little love), and it feels so incredible, it's a highly leveraged way to enhance the quality of life—for ourselves and for the good of others.

Sometimes having a special cause means volunteering a few hours a week (or even a month) or getting more involved in church- or temple-related causes. It can mean anything from helping build a house for Habitat for Humanity, to working in a soup kitchen for the homeless, to picking up litter on your street. It can mean spending time with lonely people or helping someone to learn to read. It might involve learning more about specific causes and then offering to help with money or ideas. Perhaps there is a special project at your office or at your child's school.

Having a special cause can either be structured or unstructured. It might mean mentoring a child—formally or informally—or helping to jump-start someone who has potential in your eyes. Mostly, it means doing something—anything—to be of help or of service to someone or something. It's doing something, on a regular basis, that has nothing to do with you, other than your desire to be of help. It can be done with others or alone. It can be done openly or anonymously.

What many men have discovered is that, at first, they want to be of service because it's the right thing to do. What many discover, however, is that being of service does every bit as much for them as it does for the people or cause they are helping. Being selfless, whatever form it happens to take, does wonders for the spirit. It takes you out of your own world and into our shared humanity. It takes your mind off your own problems and concerns, as it opens your heart and deepens your perspective.

Many men have told me, in letters and in person, that being of service has not only become one of the most important and nourishing aspects, but also one of the absolute highlights of their life. In fact, many cannot imagine how they lived for so long, unaware of the hidden gifts that service brings—not only to the world, but to their personal lives as well. Many men have told me that it's much easier to not sweat the small stuff when they are doing something for others.

Sometimes, men have a reputation of being a little self-centered and single-minded in terms of success. I think we should all get together and dispel this myth once and for all. There must be at least a few billion of us men here on this planet. What if each of us did just a tiny bit more for a special cause than we do right now? The result would be a phenomenal shift: not only would a lot more good be done, but in addition, the men of the world would live richer, more satisfying lives.

8

BE ABLE TO LAUGH
AT YOURSELF

The other day I was struggling with some work, taking it (and myself) a little too seriously. I needed something to help me break the tension. My timing was perfect. I flipped on an audiotape to the perfect line. The speaker, Ram Dass, said, "If you don't have a sense of humor, it just isn't funny." I almost fell out of my chair laughing at myself.

I had been unusually forgetful that day and had made a number of mistakes. At the time, it seemed like everyone was mad at me. I was taking things too personally and feeling a bit overwhelmed. But when I heard that comical line, everything changed in an instant.

When you think about it, it really is funny. Here we are, somewhat helpless, tiny little people taking on a great big world. Make no mistake about it; in my opinion, we do pretty darned well. But sometimes it's just too much. We have hundreds of things to do, tons of responsibility, people relying on us, and the moment-to-moment potential for so many things to go wrong. Yet, to our credit, we keep on trying.

But to think we can keep it going—100 percent of the time, to keep so many balls in the air, stay on top of everything, be in touch with so many people, be mistake free, and do it all with a smile—is ludicrous.

Sometimes, you just have to laugh at yourself. And when you do, it's a huge relief.

When you depersonalize life a little bit, and laugh at yourself, it takes the pressure off feeling like you have to be perfect or do it all. You're able to see the innocence in your human(ness). You're also able to be a bit easier on other people too, as you extend your lighthearted attitude in their direction. Rather than taking so many things personally and demanding such high standards, you can back off, if even a little, and give others a break. You can make allowances for the fact that we're all human—and we're all in this together.

Kids can help us remember to laugh at ourselves too. One day I walked into my older daughter's bedroom while she was talking on the phone. Trouble was, she was supposed to be doing her homework. I launched into a lecture, but she was unimpressed. Instead, she asked me, "Dad, tell me again exactly what it is that you do for a living?"

Her timing was perfect, and I couldn't help but laugh at myself. Here I was, a person who encouraged people not to sweat the small stuff, getting on her for a little thing like a phone call. Instantly, I went from being uptight and serious to having a smile on my face and taking the rest of the day in stride.

A sense of humor does many things. Not only does it make you feel less tense and anxious, but it gives you better judgment as well. Rather than being bogged down with seriousness, you're able to rise above the cloud and see things more clearly.

If you haven't yet done so, I encourage you to look yourself in the mirror and laugh out loud (respectfully, of course). You're one of a kind, a character no doubt. Why not enjoy yourself a bit more than you have in the past? My guess is, you probably enjoy people with a sense of humor more than you do people without one. By applying the same standard to yourself, you may find yourself enjoying your own company and liking yourself more than ever before.

9

DON'T LET YOUR COMPETITIVE NATURE GET THE BEST OF YOU

I haven't met many men whom I've felt weren't at least a bit competitive. And I'm all for it. Not only do we live in a competitive world, but many men have told me that they feel that their competitive nature and their ability to compete are a couple of their greatest assets.

When I suggest that, as men, we not allow our competitive natures to get the best of us, I'm not suggesting we get rid of them, but rather that we keep them in perspective. One of the most effective ways to create a happier, less stressed, and more balanced life is to remember that there is far more to life than winning and losing. And I don't say this simply as an overture or because it sounds like a good thing to put into a book on happier living. Instead, I say this because when we look back on our lives from our deathbeds—a year from now, five years, ten, twenty, fifty, or whatever—it's almost certain that the most important aspects will not have been our ability to dominate others, collect achievements, win contests, and beat out our competition.

Instead, the things that will seem most important will be the quality of our lives. We will measure the success of our lives by the type of relationships we had with ourselves and with others. We will reflect upon our children, spouse or girlfriend, relatives, friends, colleagues, and other important people in our lives. We will value qualities such as compassion, patience, generosity, and kindness. We will remember the touching moments and the heart-warming experiences.

Again, I'm not dismissing the fact that being competitive is necessary in our world—it is. Walk into any major bookstore and you'll quickly find that even an author faces stiff and extremely competent competition—every single day. But regardless of the reality or severity of the competition we face, it's up to us how we approach the subject. Obviously, there are times when being competitive is not only appropriate, but important. The question is, is being competitive everything? Does it dominate your life, your judgment, and your priorities? Do you allow it to adversely affect relationships and dominate your very existence? Or is it simply a part of who you are and how you live your life?

Keeping our competitive natures in check does wonders for your own peace of mind. It has the effect of taking the pressure off, as if to remind you that there is less on the line. Sure, you do your best to succeed—and win—at all you do, but with less sense of desperation. And when you don't succeed, or win, or get your desired result, it's not experienced as the end of the world or as a statement of your value as a person. It also allows you to let others shine or be in the limelight, and you are able to share in the joy of their success. It makes it much easier for you to "switch gears" from a competitive environment such as work, to a more peaceful environment such as home and family. Finally, it allows you to be as generous as possible to others and to the causes you believe in, without sacrificing your own success or security.

Perspective on competitiveness is an effective antidote to stress and feeling overwhelmed. I hope you'll take some time to reflect on the relative importance of being a competitive man. I think you'll come to the conclusion that, while it is important, it isn't everything.

10

LEARN ABOUT LIFE FROM GOLF

I'm not a golfer, but I sure know a lot of people who are or who want to be. It's a beautiful game, and I can certainly understand why people enjoy it so much.

I love acronyms, and the word "golf" is one of the best I've ever come across. If you put together the letters G-O-L-F, what you come up with is this: Gift Of Life Forever. If we could only remember what a gift life is, we'd surely be happier, and we wouldn't be sweating the small stuff. At least not as often.

Some professionals and experts in golf have told me that when you're playing effectively, you're completely absorbed in the moment. You're fully present. Each shot is independent from the rest. In other words, whether you strike a perfect drive or miss an easy putt, you put it out of your mind and move on. You're relaxed, yet focused. You're having fun. While you're focused on the ball, you're nevertheless aware of the beauty that surrounds you. There's a part of you that is ever grateful to be able to play such a wonderful game.

Many lovers of the game of golf have told me that when they are at their best, they are in the flow of the game. In other words, their game comes easily and effortlessly, almost like it's happening without the player. Somehow, your body knows exactly what to do. Concentration is so easy during these times that you are not easily distracted. And if you are distracted, it's easy to return to that peaceful and effective zone.

It's no wonder that people love the game of golf so much. In a way, it's symbolic of a near-perfect way of living. When playing golf, there are times that you're very strong and deliberate. Other times, you rely on a soft touch. The entire game is one of instinct.

So, too, with life itself. When we're playing the game of life well, we're in that flow golfers speak about. Life is relatively easy, and things just seem to fall into place. Ideas and solutions come to us, almost as if from out of the blue. Things happen, and we respond accordingly.

In male terminology, golf is supposed to be a gentleman's game. There are codes of ethics and behavior that are allegedly followed by all who love the game. A life well lived is played by a similar set of rules. Ethics and integrity are near the top of the priority list. Like golf, life can be extremely competitive. Yet, a professional golfer would never let his competitive nature interfere with his sportsmanship.

Patience is a virtue in both golf and in life. It's interesting to observe a good golfer eyeing his next shot. He takes his time and absorbs the totality of his environment. He waits until he is ready to take his shot. So, too, in life. Living effectively involves plenty of patience. When we are patient, opportunities present themselves and solutions tend to surface.

It's really interesting to ponder the similarities between a good game of golf and an effective life. The next time you get a chance, watch (or play) a round of golf. While you're at it, think of the deeper meaning and possible implications of the game. It's a fun, inspirational, and slightly different way to bring peace and perspective into your daily life.

11

GRANT YOURSELF ONE HOUR

Let's face it: Most of us are pressed for time, too busy, and often rushed. Few men haven't tried to convince themselves that "When I get time, I'll go ahead and do the things that I know are good for me" (for example, exercise, meditation, prayer, reading, yoga, and so forth). In other words, "I can't do it now—but later, for sure." The problem, of course, is that if you don't actually carve out the time, you'll never get around to it. Life is always busy—always has been and always will be. It's always one thing after another. Even if you get a moment here or there, it will almost surely fill up with some other obligation. That's just life.

But there is a solution. It's not perfect, but it works pretty well. I call it the one-hour solution. My thinking is this: There are twenty-four hours in a day. That's 1,440 minutes. All of us work hard for our employers, clients, families, even for the government. (I heard somewhere that the average person works from January 1 until around the middle of April just to pay his or her taxes.) Doesn't it sound reasonable that a tiny percentage (less than 5 percent) of our time could be reserved for ourselves to do something healthy? I certainly think so.

Here's how it works, in a practical sense. You make the decision that you're going to spend a total of one hour a day, say, six days a week, doing those things that nourish your body and spirit. That means a total of six hours out of the 168 in any given week. You can spend that time doing whatever you want to do, as long as it's geared toward the body/mind/spirit connection. I spend my hour doing some combination of exercise—jogging or working out at the gym, meditation, reading, yoga, or stretching. Some days I might exercise the entire hour or spend the time doing yoga and meditation, but it's always something positive, uplifting, and healthy. The only rule is that you have to spend the time away from your routine. In other words, you can't spend your hour catching up on phone calls or paperwork.

Certainly there are exceptions, but a vast majority of people can find a way to make this happen if they really want it to. I knew a lawyer who decided to skip his lunch hour three or four times a week so that he could use the time for jogging. Instead of filling up on calories, he was burning them off. He was lucky that his firm had a shower he could use. Certainly many of us don't have that luxury, but maybe there are other options. Perhaps there is a health club close to work that you could join—or a group of you could join together. I heard of a guy who used to leave for work at 7:30 and get to work by 9:00. By leaving at 6:30 instead, he missed most of the traffic and had an extra hour to exercise and meditate.

One possible objection to this idea is that it's selfish to spend a whole hour on oneself, especially every day. After all, people depend on us. When you think about it, however, you'll discover that it's not selfish at all. Remember that when you spend a little time taking care of yourself physically, emotionally, and spiritually, you become a deeper, kinder person. You become less reactive and more patient. You develop your compassion, kindness, and generosity. So that when you're with your spouse or girlfriend, children, friends, and coworkers, you'll be easier to be around—and more fun, too.

Obviously, to take one hour a day for yourself requires some discipline and sacrifice. But keep in mind the tremendous payoffs—better health and fitness, more energy, a calmer and happier spirit, a more balanced life, and so forth. You might be surprised at some of the additional perks as well—a sharper learning curve, better perspective, and increased creativity. However you look at it, it's mostly upside. I hope you'll experiment with this one—it just may change your life.

12

DON'T JUMP SHIP

Imagine, for a moment, that you are on a luxurious, extremely comfortable private yacht: perfect temperature, cruising at optimum speed, right on course to your ideal destination. Comforting music is playing at just the right volume. Everything about your experience is relaxing.

Now imagine what would happen if you left the sanctity of your peaceful yacht and jumped into the ice-cold water of the Atlantic Ocean. You'd be in shock. Your peace would be replaced with extreme discomfort and stress. You'd be miserable, struggling to get back to the comfort of the boat.

I love the metaphor of the yacht because it's a perfect analogy for what happens when we leave an effective, calm state of mind by "jumping" into a negative mode of thought. Think about it. You can be having a perfectly nice day, effective, relaxed, and relatively stress-free, when a pesky thought enters your mind. It can be practically anything: "God that guy was a jerk," "I can't believe how much work I have to do," or "I'm sick of traffic." There are an unlimited number of potential examples.

But rather than simply letting the thought pass by, taking note of it, and allowing it to drift away, like the millions of thoughts before it—you instead jump at it, study or analyze the content of the thought, and think about it some more. You get all worked up or stressed out, and become tense and bothered. How many times a day do you suppose this happens? I can't tell you for sure, but I can tell you that, even after many years of sharing this concept with others, I still catch myself engaging in this insidious habit virtually every day. It's amazing.

Simply becoming aware of this mental dynamic is extremely helpful. Once you're aware of it, here's what happens. You'll be doing fine and a stray thought will pop into your mind. You'll jump and begin to feel stressed. All of a sudden you'll see what you did, and you'll gain more perspective about it. You'll realize how easy it is to get trapped or fall prey to negativity. You might even see the humor in it.

Over time, you'll catch yourself earlier and earlier. You'll begin to feel the connection between jumping ship and feeling bad or stressed. At some point, you'll actually see it coming. You might say to yourself, "No way, I'm not going there," because you will know what will happen if you do.

Obviously, there are plenty of instances where it's appropriate and perhaps even desirable to pursue a negative thought, get mad, think through difficult topics, or even "jump ship." What this strategy does, however, is give you options and help you avoid taking this too far. It keeps you from entertaining most of the negative and destructive thoughts that drift through your mind. It helps you sort through and determine which thoughts are worth pursuing—and which ones aren't worth the trouble.

A calm mind is clever, creative, effective, and resourceful. By not jumping ship so often, you'll keep your bearings and life won't seem so difficult. Following every negative train of thought that enters your mind is stressful. Stay on board, and your life will more manageable and less exhausting. You'll have more energy for the fun things—like boating, perhaps!

13

SEE IT AS A TEST

One of my favorite funny, but thought-provoking sayings is this: "Life is a test. It is only a test. Had this been real life, you would have been instructed where to go and what to do." The first time I saw this parody of the Emergency Broadcasting System warning, I could immediately relate to it. Sometimes when life seems to get a bit too crazy, I pull this out and read it—over and over again.

There are times when a lighthearted message can be just what the doctor ordered. It can be a simple reminder that, when you think about it, life really is a series of tests, one right after another. Just when it seems as if things are going smoothly, something else seems to happen. I've always felt that one of the best strategies, especially when dealing with relatively minor "stuff," is to remember to keep your sense of humor and to not take it too seriously.

I'll never forget an instance when this saying came in really handy. I was speaking to a large group of parents about staying calm in the midst of dealing with kids and chaos. After the event, I took a long flight home, and one of my kids was getting ready to have a sleep-over that night. My girls were fighting like cats and dogs, the noise level was excessive, and the house was a complete mess. Probably because of the mood I was in,

I felt like I had walked into a circus. I could feel my peace of mind slipping away as I became more and more uptight.

After a while, I walked into my office to read the mail and check my messages. (What I was really doing, of course, was trying to escape.) As I fumbled through some papers, I came across this saying and almost laughed my head off. Indeed, what a test it was—and boy, was I failing.

Almost immediately, however, I felt better. I could see the humor of the situation. After all, that very day I had been paid to teach others how to deal with this exact type of thing—and here I was losing my cool. I shook it off and went back out to help the girls prepare for their guests.

I'm sure you can think of many instances where this bit of lighthearted wisdom would have come in handy for you, too. We've all heard the expression, "testing your patience." How often does that happen? Now you can see why it's called a "test."

The good news is that from now on, you'll have a secret weapon at your disposal. Write this message down and carry it with you. Then, the next time you're confronted with a minor hassle and you begin to get all worked up about it—pull it out. You may be pleasantly surprised at how funny it will seem. Or, if not funny, perhaps it will at least take the edge off.

I've found it really helpful to see life—especially the hassles and irritations—as a series of tests. Somehow, it puts things into better perspective, allowing me to keep my patience, see the bigger picture, and let things go more easily (at least most of them). I hope you'll give this simple suggestion a try—you'll be glad you did.

14

FLASH FORWARD
FOR INSTANT PERSPECTIVE

I was sitting with a man who was complaining about his two kids, ages nine and fourteen. He was upset with the young one because he hadn't yet developed any passion for sports. He was upset with his older child because she wasn't demonstrating any interest in good grades or any curiosity about college. It was clear that they weren't living up to his expectations, and he seemed burdened by it all.

Very gently I asked him, "Seems like yesterday they were little babies, doesn't it?" "Sure does," he replied, as his manner softened. I then asked him, "How much do you suppose you'll miss them when they leave the house in a few years and your time with them as a day-to-day parent is over?" There was a reflective pause in our conversation, followed by a further softening in his body language and words. It was almost as if he realized, perhaps for the first time, that his expectations and judgments were interfering with his ability to enjoy his kids. By skipping forward a few years, he was able to look back and see what he'd be missing.

While not everyone is able to see it so quickly, there is nonetheless something very powerful in being able to "flash forward" down the road a ways, in order to give yourself some instant perspective.

The experience of being with this man helped me to realize how often I do this in my own life. Sometimes, when I'm feeling a bit overwhelmed or burdened by my responsibilities, I'll imagine what it will be like when I no longer have those supposed burdens to complain about. I've done this many times in all different aspects of my life—personal, professional, even regarding my home. Once, when I was feeling stressed by all the time and effort it takes to keep up our yard and house, I quieted down enough to imagine what it will be like some day when I don't have a yard to care for. Suddenly, even things like gardening, weeding, and pruning seemed less daunting. I realized that it's easy to find reasons to complain about practically anything when, in reality, I'd much rather have them than not.

I was speaking to a man who used to travel a great deal for his work. He complained constantly about the travel and how stressful it was. For years he longed for a job that didn't require any travel. He finally found that job, and— you guessed it—a few months later he missed the travel. We spoke about the idea of flashing forward, after the fact. He admits that, had he spent some time doing so, prior to making his final decision, he would have made a different choice. He would have realized that there were actually plenty of things he loved about the travel.

What seems to happen to people, when they experiment with this strategy, is that they are almost forced to bring their attention back to the here-and-now. In other words, by thinking about what you'll miss later, you're reminded of what's truly important right now. What I've discovered is that many of the very things that burden and overwhelm us are the very things that we will miss most when they are gone. Acknowledging this is a very powerful and humbling insight.

I'll bet you'll have a similar response if you give this strategy a try. By flashing forward to the future, you will enhance your perspective in some powerful ways.

15

SEE STRESS AS NONSEXY

We live in a time when, on the surface, stress is glorified and celebrated. Many of us rush around bragging about how busy we are, how little sleep we get, and how long it's been since we've taken a vacation. I know a number of people who claim to have many days when they don't even have time to go to the bathroom. We attempt to impress our colleagues, spouses, girlfriends, associates, even our children with our hectic schedules. Many people I know would be embarrassed to admit they took a nap, had a day to themselves, or took time to take a daily walk or browse in a bookstore.

Yet, if you take a step back and look again, it's easy to see how being around someone who is constantly complaining about their busyness is a huge turnoff. After a while, it's downright boring to be around someone whose major topic of conversation has to do with how stressed or busy they are. How many times does someone really, truly want to hear about it? Who in their right mind would want to spend time with someone who is always frazzled and usually more interested in the next scheduled event than in their current conversation? Why would a woman share herself with a man whose life is totally out of control? Wouldn't most people— women and men—prefer to hang out with people who seem like they have time for us and who listen to us?

The very act of asking these questions is a great way to begin to your stress-reducing plan. It's much easier to get rid of something you see as a flaw than something you consider a virtue. Imagine how difficult it would be to lose weight if you glorified being 200 pounds overweight. It would be virtually impossible.

Many people confuse a reduction in their stress with apathy, or fear they might lose their edge. Nothing could be further from the truth. As your stress is reduced, your ability to focus and concentrate is enhanced. Rather than being distracted by being overwhelmed and bothered, you'll be able to remain calm in the eye of the storm. Rather than scrambling around, frantic and frenzied, you'll be peaceful and centered. You'll be a better listener, and your learning curve will sharpen.

I never thought I'd link stress and sex appeal together in the same sentence. Yet, it's helpful to see the relationship. I'm a firm believer in the "whatever works" philosophy. And since I believe that seeing this relationship can be a huge motivating force, I decided to bring it to your attention.

16

SHARE YOUR DREAMS

It's so nice to have a partner, or friends, or a family member to share your dreams with. My dream, for many years, has been to live near the ocean. And, although it hasn't happened (nor does it appear likely), it's been nice to share this dream with my partner, Kris, and several of my close friends.

Sharing your dreams is the positive, flip side of complaining. Instead of sharing your dissatisfactions and unfulfilled dreams in a negative way, which will only reinforce your own unhappiness and bring others down with you, you're instead uplifting your own spirits and those around you by sharing a dream that is in your heart.

In a strange sort of way, the act of sharing a dream takes away the compulsion to feel as though you have to have that dream fulfilled. In other words, you may really want something and dream about having it. But when you share openly, from your heart with someone who really cares, the sharing alone can sometimes be enough. The reason is that there is an inherent satisfaction that exists in the process of sharing itself.

For example, my dream to live by the ocean is very real. I love the ocean and thrive when I'm near it. I can't remember not feeling contented when I was near the water. The beauty, sounds, clean air, and atmosphere heighten my senses and make me feel good. The reality of our life, however, is such that it doesn't make a great deal of sense for us to move. We're settled in and happy where we are.

I could approach this issue in several ways. First, I could deny my dream or pretend that it doesn't exist. That would be false and would create frustrated feelings within me, perhaps even twinges of resentment for feeling stuck. The second way I could deal with it would be to complain and feel sorry for myself. I could remind Kris and my kids, often, of how unhappy I am where we are and how it isn't fair that we can't live where I want to be. That would be a guaranteed way to create anger and hostility in my family. They would either feel guilty or, more likely, angry at me for not being supportive of their choices. Finally, I could make the decision to be happy right where we are, yet, on occasion, share my dream with Kris and my family in a positive way, perhaps by taking a vacation at the beach whenever possible.

There are many practical applications of this strategy. I think the most important part of this idea is to become familiar with the 180-degree difference between complaining and sharing. For the most part, people hate to listen to complainers. They tune them out, feel sorry for them, push them away, and wish they would stop. On the other hand, it's really fun to listen to someone share a dream.

Consider how you would respond to the following two sentences spoken by a spouse, lover, or friend. First, "I hate my stupid job; it sucks." Or, "Do you know what I'd really love to be doing?" Wow—what a difference. In the first sentence, you, as the listener or receiver of the complaint, want to leave the room. Your instinct is to pull away. In the second, however, you want to hear more; you want to engage in the conversation because it brings you closer to the person who is sharing.

Sharing your dreams is a great way to clarify your desires and make peace with that which you may not be able to get or have. It's also a great way to enhance your communication and bring you closer to others. Spend some time reflecting on your own dreams. Think of your complaints and turn them into a positive experience. You may find that those closest to you will want to hear everything you have to say. I hope your dreams do come true, but even if they don't, I hope you'll be able to share them with others.

17

BE A PART OF THE SOLUTION

My dad used to say to me, "Our actions determine whether we become part of the solution—or part of the problem." And while this is a multidimensional, somewhat complex statement, deep down, I think it's absolutely true. Often, we are indeed either part of the solution or part of the problem.

I say it's complicated because, obviously, there are times when you may be part of a certain solution, but by the very nature of what you're doing, you become part of a different problem. For example, starting a business helps create jobs and contributes to certain needs, which means you're part of those solutions. On the other hand, depending on a variety of factors, you might be creating all sorts of other problems: traffic, parking, the heavy use of natural resources, additional pollution, to name just a few.

Even something like the decision to have a large family has its own pros and cons, in terms of the big picture. On the one hand, you are part of the solution in terms of bringing more loving, capable people into our world. However, you're part of the problem in terms of increasing our already large population.

The real point, however, has to do with the day-to-day, moment-to-moment choices we make and the way we live our lives. For example, if you choose to keep your consumption at a reasonable level, conserve energy when it's practical to do so, and recycle as best you can, you're part of the environmental solution. If you couldn't care less, and you leave all your lights and appliances on, even when you leave the house, never recycle, and so forth, you're part of the problem.

If you are able to do so, and you contribute at least some portion of your time, energy, or money to a favorite cause, church, organization, or charity, then you're part of the "reduce suffering" solution. If your only concern is your own wants and needs, you probably aren't much help in this category.

In a general sense, if you treat people with respect, run an ethical business, pay people generously, forgive easily, take responsibility for your own actions, and admit when you've made a mistake, then you're part of the solution in terms of creating a kinder, better, more ethical world. If these things have no value in your mind, well, then you might be part of the problem.

All of us are a part of certain solutions and a part of other problems. The value of reflecting on this issue is that it gives us a chance to take an honest look and to assess where we are in terms of our own contribution to humanity, compared to where we might want to be. Personally, I've found that it can be a real eye-opening exercise and can encourage some really powerful, positive changes in one's life.

I brought up this idea during one of my talks to an organization. After the lecture, a man came up to me and said, "I want to thank you for bringing this issue to my attention." He said that while he has always thought of himself as a really nice guy—and "quite generous"—the truth was that he was giving away less than half of 1 percent of his income.

He said, "I wasn't being ungenerous on purpose; I simply hadn't thought much about it."

I've had similar insights about my own life. For example, while I'm careful not to waste certain resources, I've discovered that I can be quite wasteful in other areas. Because I'm now more aware of it, I'm working on becoming less a part of those problems and more a part of the solution.

Personally, I think this strategy can play an important role in self-assessment. It's not a big deal, and it's not meant to make us feel bad, guilty, or inadequate. It is there, however, to give us a chance to decide for ourselves whether we are part of the problem or part of the solution—and whether we want to do something about it. I've found that my own stress level has decreased and my happiness has increased as a result of knowing that I'm doing the best I can to be a part of as many solutions as possible.

18

GIVE 'EM A BREAK

So often when we're sweating the small stuff, it has to do with other people. We're annoyed, irritated, bothered, impatient, or simply don't understand why someone is behaving (or not behaving) the way we feel they should.

Yesterday, I brought my girls to a restaurant and witnessed a man complaining, in an argumentative tone, about his service. He was rolling his eyes, as if to say, "What an incompetent bunch of jerks." He was taking what he perceived to be poor service personally. What he didn't take into consideration was that his waitress was serving a dozen tables. The restaurant was very crowded and seemed to be understaffed that day. The waitress was moving very quickly and from my perspective, all things considered, she was doing a pretty good job. To me, he was the one being a jerk.

I saw a similar lack of patience the other day at the airport. People were angry, taking out their frustration on the ticket agents, sometimes in a verbally abusive manner. It was as if no one was taking into consideration the weather problems around the country or the air traffic safety concerns.

The problem is that everyone else's job looks so easy—only ours seems really difficult. However, if you want to be a happier person, it's critical to remember two things. First, certainly not all, but most people really are doing the best that they can. Really, they are. If you get to know people and take the time to ask them, most will tell you they take pride in their work and they knock themselves out to perform well.

The second thing to remember is that almost everything is more difficult and complicated than it looks.

It can be very humbling to imagine—really imagine—having someone else's job. Just for a moment, put yourself in someone else's shoes— the ticket agent, waiter, schoolteacher, hotel reservation agent, telephone operator, flight attendant, or air traffic control operator. Each job has unique challenges and plenty of hassles.

I once overheard an interesting conversation between a highly paid executive and another person. The executive was complaining about the stress of his job and the demands on his time. The other person pointed out that real stress would be being unable to put food on the table for your children. The executive seemed to pause and reflect, which was nice to observe.

To me, there's no doubt that the executive does have a stressful job. But I think it's easy to forget that other people also have stressful lives and demands and pressures that we can't even begin to imagine. Reminding ourselves of this fact is a real gift because it gives us perspective. It helps us become more patient and forgiving and allows us to make allowances for the fact that we're all just human beings doing the best we can to live together. We have very different circumstances as well as different talents, callings, and faults—but deep down, we're pretty similar.

The next time you feel compelled to bawl someone out or judge them too harshly, take a deep breath and remember to "give 'em a break." Who knows, maybe the next time you perform less than perfectly, someone will give you a break, too.

1 9

KEEP YOUR PERSPECTIVE

I was talking to a small group of men who had been reading one of my books about various ways to keep the little things from bugging us so much. The subject of perspective came up, and one of the people shared with me the following story. I thought it was a perfect illustration of keeping one's perspective and worth sharing with you.

He said that a few weeks earlier he was in his fancy new car on his way to meet a friend for breakfast. While driving, he noticed an irritating flashing light on his dashboard. He said, "The darn thing wouldn't stop." He found himself very irritated with his car and the company that made the car. "After all," he said, "the car was only two months old." He vowed to never again buy such a "piece of junk."

He spent the entire drive thinking about it. He became increasingly agitated and imagined the upcoming telephone call where he would be chewing out the service department. He was furious that he was going to have to spend his valuable time returning to the dealership and renting another car while they fixed his.

As he drove up to the restaurant, he saw his friend entering the front door. Then it hit him! His friend didn't own a car, and, in fact, had never owned one. Instead, he had taken the bus and walked the rest of the way to meet him. In that particular instant, he gained a new perspective. As if for the first time, he realized that a vast majority of people on this earth would never experience the privilege or convenience of owning their own automobile—and that many will never ride in one. He said, "But here I was freaking out about a tiny, nonserious computer glitch that didn't even affect the performance of the car."

That's perspective in a nutshell. His story opened the door to a very interesting conversation that went on for quite some time. The man who shared the story went on to say that the insight he had had that day had lasted. In fact, he felt it was changing his life. He was beginning to catch himself getting all uptight about things that, in reality, weren't really that big a deal. The very fact that he was catching himself doing this was helping him to get over things much quicker. Someone would make a mistake or say the wrong thing, for example, and instead of blowing up, he would let it go.

This isn't to suggest that you should pretend that you love it when your car acts up—or breaks down. That would be ridiculous. Nor is it to say that you shouldn't be slightly irritated. The question is, Why so irritated? Why does something that is truly little and solvable, and that will certainly pass in time, have to ruin our day or affect our peace of mind?

Keeping things such as problems, hassles, and inconveniences in perspective is a gift. It helps you avoid unnecessary stress and heartache. The key to getting started is to take a step back and try to see the bigger picture. Ask yourself, "In the scheme of things, does this really matter?" Sometimes it does matter. But often it doesn't.

I think you'll find that the slightest shift in perspective will result in a tremendous amount of inner peace. By keeping small things small—and saving your reactions for the truly bigger things—you'll spend less time being upset and more time enjoying life.

20

SPEND TIME WITH YOUR BUDDIES

A number of married women (as well as a number of women in nonmarried but serious relationships) have told me that, once their relationship became committed, their husband or boyfriend rarely, if ever, spends time with his good friends. Many men have shared that same observation. Other than meeting for an occasional beer or to watch a ball game, or for an even more occasional activity—bowling, tennis, or fishing—it seems that most men simply give up their friendships once they become involved with a significant other.

What a shame. I can't even begin to describe what a blessing my close friendships have meant to my life. I'm not talking about meeting for a beer (although that can be a part of it too), but rather that my male friendships are, and have been, a source of inspiration, growth, comfort, and fun.

At least once every couple of months, I'll meet a close friend for a few days—just the two of us. We'll get away from our day-to-day activities and spend some treasured time together. Sometimes we plan our trip around a certain activity, skiing or fishing, for example, but mostly the time is spent just hanging out.

Our time together gives us a chance to share and reflect on life, as well as to simply hang out and do fun things. We laugh, tell stories, occasionally offer advice, and do a lot of listening.

Some men have told me, "My wife (or girlfriend) would never let me do that," seeming to suggest that there would be something wrong with doing so. My observation, however, has been that this fear comes for the most part from women whose partners have never given it a try or from men who are simply imagining that their partner would freak out or disapprove.

I'm sure there are exceptions, but if you talk to women (including my own wife, Kris) whose husbands actually do spend time with their buddies, many of them actually encourage it. They understand how important this time is, not only for their guy, but for their relationship as well. On occasion, a few days away (especially without feeling guilty or hassled) does wonders for the human spirit. I can't remember a single time that I've spent time with my close friends that I didn't return home with a heightened sense of appreciation for Kris, for my kids, and for my entire life. I'm certain—beyond any doubt whatsoever—that I'm a better person, writer, husband, and father because I allow myself this privilege. What's more, I'm happier, too. Even my kids notice a difference. I'll say to them, "I'm going to spend a few days with Benjamin (their godfather)," and one of them will say, "That's cool, Dad. Have fun! Don't forget to tell Ben that I love him."

All of us—men and women—are multidimensional. We have a variety of needs, including time for ourselves and time with our friends. It has always seemed to me that to deny this fact of life is to deny ourselves a true blessing and source of joy. And for most of us, one single person (a girlfriend or wife), regardless of how wonderful they are, cannot fulfill all of our friendship needs.

One word of caution, however. If you see the value in spending time with your good friends, keep in mind that it works both ways. Women, just like men, need special time with their friends, as well. I've met men who jump at the chance to get away with their friends, but who complain, sometimes bitterly, when their partner wants to do the very same thing. They forget: Wives and girlfriends are not possessions. We are privileged to share our lives with them, but they, like us, need and deserve other friendships.

Most of us are really busy, and our lives are filled with tons of responsibility. On the other hand, there are 365 days in a year, and my guess is that deep down, you're aware of how important your friends are to the health of your spirit. Why not try to spend at least a small portion of your time with your really good friends? Even if you can't (or don't want to) go away for days at a time, consider meeting your friends for a meal or a nature hike—not once a year, but on a somewhat regular basis. By valuing, prioritizing, and nourishing your deepest friendships, you'll rediscover one of the greatest gifts life has to offer.

21

PRACTICE MINDFULNESS

Although I'm an absolute beginner in the practice and art of mind-fulness, I can't say enough about the value it has brought to my life. I would describe mindfulness as the practice of waking meditation. It's about becoming fully alive, immersed in and awake to the present moment. Becoming more mindful allows you to be more touched by life; more grateful to be alive. It gives you the experience of a more peaceful mind and a calm, centered feeling. It also allows you to appreciate the little things instead of being bothered and stressed by so many of them.

Mindfulness is very simple, yet (at least for me) not necessarily an easy process. To me, it means being totally aware of what you're doing, while you're doing it. That sounds very simple, but give it a try and you'll see that it's a bit more difficult than that. It means that, for instance, when you're breathing, you're consciously aware that you are breathing. You feel your breath going in and out. When you're listening to someone, you're really listening. And while you're listening, you're aware that you're doing so—every moment. You don't let your mind wander—and, if it does, you gently bring it back to this moment, the moment of listening. Again, if you give this some practice, you'll be amazed at what you discover. I've had some very successful, highly charged and energized men tell me that mindfulness has been the most important thing they have ever learned in their entire life.

Even something really mundane—like cleaning the garage, for example—can be done mindfully. This means that, rather than daydreaming the entire time you are moving stuff around, sorting and cleaning, you are instead totally aware, at every moment, that you are cleaning the garage. As hard as it may be to imagine, this has the effect of turning ordinary events such as this into extraordinary experiences. It's as if you are bringing them to life. By learning to be mindful, I have learned to appreciate, rather than dread, many daily tasks and responsibilities.

The idea, as I understand it, is to bring a sense of meditation into your day-to-day, moment-to-moment activities. The way you spend your time doesn't change, but your subtle awareness level of what you are doing at any given moment is enhanced and brought to life. By being more focused, you also become more effective.

Mindfulness is also about being aware of the thoughts you have while they are emerging. Again, it sounds easy, but it's not. All of us tend to have thought after thought—in fact, to get lost in our thoughts—but not even to be aware that we are having them. If you think about it, it's almost as though we are asleep while we are awake.

Something wonderful begins to happen, however, when we are able to recognize and acknowledge our thoughts, even as they happen. The experience I've had is that a thought will surface and, rather than resist it, I'll simply acknowledge it and let it go. Even if the thought is one of fear, anger, or anxiety, I feel less compelled to react to it than I used to. Instead of freaking out or overreacting, I'm sometimes able to say, "There's a worrisome thought," and then let it go. This has nothing to do with pretending or denying. Instead, it's about being more at peace with what's really going on. Try it yourself, and you may be surprised at how powerful this simple process can be.

My personal favorite guide to mindfulness is a simple and absolutely beautiful book called *The Miracle of Mindfulness* by the Zen master Thich Nhat Hanh, who was nominated for the Nobel Peace Prize in 1967 by Martin Luther King. I refer to it often and can honestly say it has made my life easier and more peaceful. If you're at all interested in learning more, I encourage you to read this book and others on the subject.

22

LOOK AT WHAT THE CAT
DRAGGED IN

Have you ever heard the expression, "Look at what the cat dragged in?" It's meant to be funny, but it refers to someone walking through the door who doesn't look so good. Maybe the person was hung over or had had no sleep the night before. They simply look bad for one reason or another. It's the same as saying, "Yuck, look at that."

I like to use this phrase in a different, and I believe, far more constructive way. I use it to remind myself—after the fact—of the thoughts I have allowed into my mind that are only serving to bring me down or make me crazy. It's a lighthearted way to invite those types of thoughts to turn around and walk out the door the same way they came in.

For example, a thought will pop into my mind, such as, "I'm so mad at that person," or any of a thousand others. Now that it's come up, I have essentially two choices. I can entertain the thought, give it significance, and think about it some more. I can validate my reasons why I should be and think I have a right to be mad, therefore building it up into something even bigger. We all know how easy this is to do. Or, I can admit that to invite the thought to come on in is not too much different from allowing your cat to enter your front door with whatever it is he caught in the bushes.

Obviously, if there's a specific reason you want to entertain a certain thought, or if it's going to be helpful in some way, then by all means, invite it in to stay. What I'm referring to, however, are the huge numbers of angry, frustrated, or stressed-out thoughts that seem to appear out of the blue for no apparent reason other than to encourage us to get caught up in anger, stress, frustration, or some other negative emotion.

I've found this metaphor to be quite helpful. Despite being a person who has dedicated a great deal of time and energy to the subjects of happiness and attitude, I nevertheless notice random thoughts of anger, stress, worry, bother, irritation, and all the rest, popping into my mind on a regular basis. What I've found is that while I don't have as much control over which thoughts come to mind as perhaps I'd like, I do have a great deal of control over which thoughts I give significance to—and which ones I invite into "my house." By applying this somewhat graphic standard, I've found that it's pretty easy to justify kicking certain thoughts out the door.

I encourage you to give this strategy a try. As any type of thought that stresses you out enters your mind, ask yourself a very important question: Is this thought worth entertaining, or is it more like something the cat dragged in? As silly as the question might seem, you might find yourself turning some of those thoughts away—for good.

23

DO AT LEAST ONE REALLY NICE, SMALL THING FOR SOMEONE, AT LEAST ONCE A WEEK

I asked a group of (mostly) men to raise their hands and let me know when was the last time they did something really nice for someone, just to do it, with nothing expected in return. I was a bit surprised to discover that most men had trouble thinking of what it would have been, at least recently.

I then changed the subject and asked the group to think of the fondest memories of their lifetime. Not surprisingly, virtually everyone spoke of some incident having to do with pure kindness. The memories that came to mind were of times that acts of kindness were witnessed or experienced, or they had to do with times when they themselves were kind.

Without exception, every story or example was something really small and very simple. No one stood up and said, "I remember the time I set up a charitable trust" or "It was the time I wrote a large check to charity." Instead, it was things like, "I remember the time I gave up my seat on an oversold airplane so that a man could get home to his daughter's birthday." Or, "I'll never forget the time that I bit my tongue when I was about to correct my friend who made a mistake when sharing a story. It would have ruined his moment, so I let it go."

The message was clear: It's the little things having to do with kindness that matter most. When we engage in little acts of kindness, it feels good and makes us happier. The question is, If little acts of kindness make our own lives better and do some good for someone else, why in the world don't we do more of it?

Maybe we should. As an experiment, consider making a commitment to yourself to do something nice for someone, at least once a week. It's helpful to actually write it into your calendar. Make it a priority. You'll be amazed at two things. First, you'll be amazed at how easy it is; and second, you'll be amazed at how good it feels.

The act itself can be any little thing. You can, for example, pay the toll of the car behind you on the expressway or toll bridge. Or you can write a nice note or e-mail to someone, for no other reason than to say, "I was thinking of you." You can send someone flowers, even if it's not for romantic reasons. Or pull out your checkbook and take the time to write out a check to the cause of your choice. If money's tight, make the check for a small amount.

If you can't think of something nice to do for someone else, there are plenty of things you can do, on a small scale, that are just nice things to do. One of the things I like to do is to pick up at least ten pieces of litter each day. It might be in front of a store, or in your office parking lot, or along the street. I'd guess it takes all of twenty seconds and it's certainly no big deal—but every single time I do it, I feel a tiny bit better. I've found, as have many men I've spoken to, that doing an occasional nice thing, small as it might be, acts sort of like a reset button. It has the effect of helping us to remember to keep our perspective.

Another idea is to leave a voice mail message for your wife or girlfriend, telling her you'll be doing something she doesn't like to do for the next few days (dishes, cooking, laundry, shopping, driving the kids, watering the grass—whatever).

There are 1,440 minutes in a day and more than 10,000 minutes in a week. Most of us do dozens, maybe even hundreds of things in any given day. Why not take a minute or two out of those 10,000-plus and spend it doing something that will probably bring you as much or more joy than everything else combined? This strategy is a lot of fun. Once you get used to it, you might want to suggest to your friends that they give it a try as well.

24

AVOID "AS IF" ASSUMPTIONS

I heard a speaker, George Pransky, discuss this topic many years ago, and found it to be of tremendous benefit. In fact, of all the various ways I've looked at reducing stress and becoming happier, there's no question that this has been one of the most effective for me personally. I think it's particularly relevant to men, since we tend to make a lot of assumptions.

"As if" assumptions are cleverly disguised as absolute reality. They are the assumptions we make about our responses to things that happen. For example, we might operate "as if" it's necessary to be disappointed, simply because something didn't turn out the way we wanted it to. We don't see any other possible way of responding. We assume that not getting what we want equals disappointment, in the same way that fire is related to heat. Yet once you see that these types of assumptions aren't necessarily carved in stone, you open the door to a world of new possibilities.

"As if" assumptions are tricky to overcome because they seem so real and clear-cut. And some of the assumptions we make are, in fact, accurate. For example, we can assume that if we hit our finger with a hammer, it's going to hurt. Or we can assume that if we jump into a swimming pool, we're going to get wet. These assumptions are based on absolute truths— every single time. The trick is to be able to determine which "as if" assumptions are absolutely true and which ones are open to a different interpretation.

The point is this: In our minds, we create absolute, point-to-point, cause-and-effect assumptions about things when, in fact, there's really nothing holding those assumptions in place other than our own thinking. It's not as if they are carved in stone or as if someone put a gun to our head and said, "If this happens, you must react this way"—but we act as if we have absolutely no options. We'll say, "I have to feel this way; after all, such and such happened."

Let me give you a few everyday examples of these "as if" assumptions. After becoming familiar with these, you'll probably be able to see some of your own. Here's one: It's common to operate as if it's necessary to feel like a failure if you don't make as much money this year as you did last year. We assume we must feel bad, worried, and as if something is wrong. It's also popular to operate as if the only possible way to respond to losing something—a tennis game, a business deal, whatever—is to feel dejected. Watch any sports team on television after a defeat, and it's easy to believe that there simply is no other alternative—after all, their team lost. It's almost like a silent agreement that the only appropriate and possible reaction to losing is a long face, tears, and negativity.

The idea is to begin to question the validity of the "as if" assumptions that are in your life. That's it. Just begin to question them. It's not necessary to pretend you enjoy losing—very few of us do—or that you are thrilled that your financial year wasn't what you had hoped it would be. Nor is it at all necessary to say or act like you don't care or that you won't try even harder next time. This strategy isn't about pretending. It's about becoming aware that some of the assumptions we make aren't absolutely necessary. It's possible, for example, to work hard, make a certain amount of money—and be satisfied or at least not bummed out. That doesn't mean you don't want to make more next year or that you don't try to do so. Likewise, it's possible to play a game—try hard, have fun, do all you can to win—and yet, if you lose, still be happy. It's possible to be able to let it go immediately, and get on with your life.

To become aware of "as if" assumptions is very freeing. It helps you get over things much more quickly, and it enables you to let go of so many things that used to drive you nuts. On occasion, it even works on really big things. Here's an example.

I met a man whose wife had an affair. He freaked out and wanted a divorce. He was about to take permanent legal action when he heard about "as if" assumptions. He was curious. It was pointed out to him that he was operating as if the only possible response to an affair is divorce; it must ruin your life, and you must immediately end your relationship with your spouse.

Amazingly, he was able to see what his assumptions were doing to him. He realized that, painful as it was, divorce wasn't necessarily the only possible response. That tiny little openness allowed him to see the possibility that there might be another way. In this case, that's all it took to open the door to healing. He and his wife entered marriage counseling and were able to get beyond the affair. That doesn't mean he was condoning the affair, that he would put up with another one, that it wasn't painful, and so forth. It only means that he realized that there could be another way of reacting.

Becoming aware of your "as if" assumptions is not a panacea. It won't make all of your pain, stress, or frustration go away. Sometimes you'll still be upset or stressed out. However, you'll probably be able to see that being aware of your "as if" assumptions is far better than not being aware of them. There's no question in my mind that being aware of "as if" assumptions can make our lives a whole lot easier. I hope you'll agree.

25

BE CAREFUL OF
THE COMPARISON TRAP

I was speaking at a conference in Hawaii. After the event, I had a few hours free and decided to do some snorkeling. Under the water, there were thousands of beautiful fish, huge sea turtles, and incredible coral. When I finally got out of the water, I was bubbling with enthusiasm. I felt like a kid again.

As I was returning the snorkel and mask that I had borrowed, I struck up a conversation with another tourist. He was also wearing a swimsuit, and I assumed he had been snorkeling as well. I said, "Wasn't that amazing under the sea?" With a very nonchalant look on his face, he replied, "No, I didn't go in this time. It's so much better in the Bahamas."

I thought he was kidding and almost laughed out loud before I realized he was dead serious. He was so busy comparing experiences—deciding which ones were better than others—that he was missing out on one of the most beautiful and spectacular underwater sights in the entire world. His rationale was that if something wasn't "as good" or an experience didn't rate as high on his imagined scale as something else, then it clearly wasn't worth experiencing at all.

To me, that would be like saying if you had four children and one of them was a little bit better soccer player than his brothers and sisters, then you might as well not bother attending their games. Or if you had a chance to visit a great restaurant, you'd better decline, because the wine list at another restaurant is clearly superior.

Although it seemed funny at the time (and may to you too), it's really not very funny. In fact, the man in Hawaii was caught up in a common mentality that I call "the comparison trap."

Ordinarily, of course, the comparison trap plays out in far more subtle ways. Instead of missing out on underwater adventures, we stress ourselves in different types of ways. We might, for example, feel disappointed that we don't make as much money as a friend or that we can't afford the type of car that someone else can. Or we trap ourselves with comparisons from days gone by. We'll compare this year's performance with last year's, or our upcoming vacation to the one we took three years ago. I recently heard someone do just that. While in the airport waiting lounge, she said to her husband, "We'll never be able to top Europe," as if topping your previous vacation is what it's all about.

Unfortunately, when you're busy comparing one person to another or one experience to something else, you often miss out on what's right before you. Likewise, when you break the comparison habit, or at least lessen its grip on the way you see your world, you'll begin to notice that life really is a magical adventure. Each experience is unique and worthy, just the way it is.

Luckily, being trapped by comparisons is nothing more than a habit— a way of thinking about life. The solution is quite simple: Stop doing it. Easier said than done, of course, but not by too much. Once you catch yourself comparing one thing to another, it's pretty easy to start backing off. I've found that by seeing the humor in this attitude—and being able to laugh at myself a little—I'm able to drop the comparisons most of the time. When our kids were very little, I was confused once as to why our youngest wasn't acting the way her sister did when she was that same age. In a loving, but sarcastic tone, Kris reminded me, "Richard, she's a different person, remember?"

It's probably the case that most of your comparisons are harmless. On the other hand, there's no sense in robbing yourself of the enjoyment each experience has to offer. Pay attention to your comparisons, and you will find more joy in life than you ever thought possible.

26

TAKE UP YOGA

I've written about the benefits of yoga in earlier books, but I believe that its advantages are particularly important for men. I say this because, for the most part, men are real "doers"; we're proactive in the sense of wanting to do something in order to get somewhere. We're strivers and searchers, and often our minds are far removed from the present in favor of focusing on the future.

Yoga is tremendous in this regard because it's something physical that you do, yet at the same time what it does is bring your awareness back to your body and breath. It allows you to take a few moments to receive, for a change—to become filled up with positive energy and genuine inner peace.

Although I've been practicing yoga for many years, I'm still a real beginner. One of the things I love about yoga, however, is that it's perfectly okay to be a beginner, forever. It's not about getting good at it or becoming an expert, unless that's something you want to do. Instead, yoga is about experiencing your body and mind in the present moment. It's one of the only things I do in which I get to feel the benefits instantly, every single time I do it. Yoga works with the breath and includes various stretching, lengthening, and relaxing poses that combine to give you a feeling of tremendous peace in your mind and body.

I've suffered from back pain ever since my competitive tennis days in college. When I take the time to practice yoga, however, my pain is almost always under control. Similarly, no matter how many deadlines I'm under, how many planes I'm running to catch, or how much stress is present in my life, if I take the time to do yoga, it always seems manageable. I can be uptight and rushed and feeling tremendous discomfort when I start my yoga routine. Yet, by the time I finish, I feel calm, relaxed, and pain-free.

I'm writing this strategy after spending twenty minutes practicing yoga. My body feels loose and relaxed, and I feel peaceful and happy. Even though I have a lot going on today, I'm relatively certain I'm going to have a really good day. Yoga doesn't guarantee this is going to happen, but it sure increases the odds in my favor.

There are many ways to learn yoga. There are classes in many cities and books in stores and libraries. Personally, I'm a little too lazy to take the time to attend a regular class, so I either practice yoga alone or with the help of a video. You can find instructional videos at many nature, health, or sports-oriented stores, or by ordering them through yoga magazines.

I can't emphasize enough the positive influence that yoga has had in my life and in the lives of so many people I've met over the years. My guess is that, if you give it a try, you'll be hooked as well.

27

SCHEDULE TIME FOR YOUR

I was talking to a friend of mine and asked him when was the last time he went away somewhere—or spent an entire day or even part of a day—all alone, just for fun. There was dead silence.

I started asking around and quickly realized that my friend wasn't alone in his lack of alone time. In fact, virtually every man I spoke to, especially those engaged in some type of career and/or who were raising a family, fell into the same category.

Many men have become so out-of-touch with spending time alone that some, when asked the question, would respond with, "Why would I want to do that?" Let me answer that question.

You live with yourself twenty-four hours a day, 365 days a year. To get to know anyone (even yourself) requires some time and attention. It's not the same, however, when you're immersed in your work, family, and other responsibilities. Imagine trying to get to know someone, perhaps in a new relationship, but never spending any quiet time alone. Every time you're together, there are two or three other people with you, phones ringing, and responsibilities to attend to. Your chances of really getting to know that person intimately would be zero. You'd know them on the surface, but not at a deeper level.

The same applies to yourself. In order to get to know yourself, you just spend some time with yourself, hang out, take some walks, engage in some reflection. And not just once or twice, but on a somewhat regular basis.

So what's the value of knowing yourself? Well, for one, you can't like someone unless you know them. And if you don't like yourself, there are so many negative ramifications. In addition, you can't take care of them very well because you don't really know their specific needs. I've always thought that one of the reasons many men have midlife crises is that it suddenly hits them that they really don't know themselves very well, if at all.

It's amazing what can happen to a man when he gives himself permission to spend some time alone. It gives you a chance to think, quietly and without distraction. You can reflect on your life—what you like and don't like—things you'd like to do, dreams you have, activities you'd like to try, and ways you'd like to grow and improve as a person. Being alone gives you a break, a chance to breathe and to lighten up. I met a man who told me that spending time alone has helped him to realize that he loved his wife more than he ever realized. He had been frustrated for years. Being away, even for very short periods of time, created the space he needed to feel reconnected. I have a similar experience virtually every time I get away. I return with feelings of gratitude for my wife and children.

Being away, alone, can take many forms. It can be anything from taking a drive through the country for a few hours on a Saturday, to going fishing or some other solitary adventure for several days, or more. One additional note, however: Although it can be fun, a trip filled with too much stimulus—gambling, partying, and stuff like that—isn't what I'm talking about. Those types of outings are too distracting.

Sometimes the biggest obstacle to going away alone can be your relationship with your wife or girlfriend. At times, people can feel threatened when their partner expresses a need for some space. I can only say two things about that objection. First, if you're at all like me, your partner will be thrilled when you return because you'll be easier to be around, happier and more fun. Whenever we first meet our own emotional needs, our natural instinct is to reach out and be more loving to those we care about. Second, if this were a book for women, I'd be making the same suggestion. My wife, Kris, feels exactly the same way I do, and we each encourage the other to spend time alone. Incidentally, she also covers this in her book, *Don't Sweat the Small Stuff for Women*.

Even if you start very small—an hour or two at a time—I hope you'll explore this idea. You'll feel less stressed, happier, and my guess is, you'll love it more than you can possibly imagine.

28

GET OUT OF THE SERIOUS MODE

I admit it. There are times when I get way too serious about life, and I begin to allow myself to get overwhelmed and uptight. It happened just the other day—and Kris came to the rescue.

I had just returned from a business trip where I had been speaking. The event went well, but it had put me behind on what felt like a truck-load of responsibility. I became helpless and overwhelmed, feeling as if I had hundreds of things to do. There were stacks of unreturned phone calls, requests, and other demands on my time. I had several deadlines to meet and wasn't sure where the time was going to come from. In addition, we were having some construction work done on our home, and the noise didn't help my concentration. I had a horrible backache and, to top it off, my daughters were having one of those sister fights. You know the story—blah blah blah.

Kris could see that I had lost perspective, and she asked me to sit down with her for a minute. In a funny, but nevertheless respectful tone, she said, "Hmmm, do you think it's possible you might be taking it all a bit too seriously this morning? Isn't there any part of this that seems funny?"

That's all it took to make me smile and even chuckle a little. The truth was, as it so often is, that it was simply one of those mornings that everyone has every once in a while. With the tiniest bit of humor I was able to see that things weren't quite as bad as I was imagining them to be and that everything would be okay.

There is something freeing about being able to differentiate between a normal state of mind and a stressed-out or serious mode. While you're stressed, you usually have thoughts like, "No one understands how busy I am," "I have it really tough," or "I'll never get through this one." If you're like me, you feel a little sorry for yourself and rush around reminding yourself (and others) how much there is to do. Everything is exaggerated and seems to be falling apart.

Yet, if you can have the slightest sense of humor about it—just enough to recognize what you're doing—it makes all the difference. Admitting to yourself that you're in a serious mode allows you to peek over the edge or gather just a tiny bit of perspective. Then you're able to see that perhaps it's not quite as bad as you're making it out to be. Don't get me wrong: I know these situations feel confusing and stressful. But when you acknowledge the fact that you're in the serious mode, it lightens your spirits just enough to be helpful.

Once you see yourself in the serious mode, you can lighten up enough to see yourself as a character again. You'll see a glimpse of humor in the craziness of it all. This feeds your perspective, which, in turn, makes everything seem a bit more manageable. At the very least you'll be able to get back on track, take it one step at a time, and get on with your day.

Whether you're lucky enough to have someone point it out to you, or whether you have to see it for yourself, be open to the possibility that the serious mode gives you the illusion that life is coming to an end—

that it's all too much—when in fact, all that's happening is that you're having a bad day. The next time you get too serious, lighten up. More likely than not, all will be okay.

29

THINK "MAYBE SO, MAYBE NOT"

One of the reasons it's so easy to get stressed and uptight has to do with the fact that we are often so certain in our positions and assumptions. Rather than maintaining a degree of openness to the unknown—openness to the possibility that things may work out just fine—we instead convince ourselves that we not only know what's going to happen, but also that, whatever "it" is, it's going to be horrible. So we tense up, clench our fists, and prepare for battle. The problem is, it's often totally unnecessary. In other words, we often stress ourselves out over nothing.

Jim's fourteen-year-old son, Ryan, was having a tough time in school, socially and academically. Just when he thought things couldn't get any worse, Ryan's only really good friend announced that he was moving. "That's it," Jim thought to himself, "this will be the final straw that breaks my son's back."

You probably know the rest of the story. It turned out that Ryan and his friend, despite being great buddies, were actually keeping each other back, so to speak. He was so attached to his only friend, that he wasn't reaching out to anyone else. By losing his friend, he was forced to expand his circle. His new friends were better students and even nicer people, which rubbed off on Ryan. His grades improved, as did his ultimate happiness and growth as a teenager. Again, what appeared tragic turned out to be nothing more than a necessary speed bump. This doesn't mean it wasn't painful—it was, but it wasn't the end of the world.

There is something very powerful and encouraging about the willingness to stay open to possibilities and being humble enough to admit that, in reality, we really don't know what's going to happen. We can guess, make reasonable assumptions, and predict—but we don't know for sure. In fact, often something that appears to be negative turns out to be positive, or vice versa. I remember wanting to attend a certain college many years ago, but I didn't have the grades to get in. On the surface, this appeared negative. It didn't turn out that way at all. In my second year, I ended up being the top tennis player on the men's varsity team, being selected as team captain, and maturing a great deal before transferring to Pepperdine University, where I met Kris. Had I been admitted to my first choice, chances are none of this would have happened.

The same scenario exists in so many aspects of life. A girl you adore leaves you—but you find someone who's even better for you. You get laid off—and this leads to your finding the perfect career. You get transferred to a new location and you're devastated to leave your friends. Shortly thereafter, however, you meet the best friend you've ever known. It happens all the time. It looks horrible; it feels horrible. You're certain it's horrible—but it turns out to be fine.

Thinking "maybe so, maybe not" is not the same as being apathetic or wishy-washy. Nor is it phony. It's not like you're going to walk around acting thrilled when something painful happens or that you're going to pretend that you're happy when you're not. It's simply a matter of recognizing and admitting that things are very often not as they seem at first glance. And because this is true, it makes a great deal of sense to be less reactive and panicked when something appears problematic. Obviously, you're always going to do everything you can to solve as well as prevent problems, and you're always going to put all the odds in your favor whenever possible. Yet, what's the point of assuming the worst, getting stressed, overwhelmed, and pessimistic, when the real truth is that the end result is unknown.

I'll admit to being somewhat of an optimist. Yet, if you think about it, I've got history on my side: Life, as well as its many ups, downs, and problems, tends to work itself out. Proof of that is that you're here today—right now. So the next time something appears to be a huge problem, stay open to the possibility that it might not be as horrible as you imagine it to be. Say the words, "Maybe so, maybe not." Who knows? It could even be a blessing in disguise.

30

DON'T LET THE "TURKEYS"
GET YOU DOWN

I believe this topic is so important that, a few years ago, I was going to write an entire book with this title. Eventually, I decided that instead of an entire book, I would wait for the perfect opportunity to include a few thoughts on the subject in an appropriate *Don't Sweat* book. That time is now.

As I reflect on my own life, talk to friends and acquaintances, and meet people all over the world, it's clear to me that one of the biggest challenges we face—of a relatively small nature—is to not let extremely difficult people (that is, turkeys) get us down.

I'm writing these words while sitting in the Burbank, California, airport. I just returned my rental car to a grumpy, impatient employee. There are hundreds of people around me, and most of them seem to be in an enormous hurry. A small percentage are smiling or laughing; the rest seem to be agitated and stressed.

As I sat down, a middle-aged man pushed a woman out of the way to secure his place in line before her. He then began to talk on his cell phone. His voice was loud and disruptive, and he was soon in an argument with the person he was speaking to. A woman in front of the same line was being extremely argumentative with the ticket agent. She seemed to think it was the ticket agent's fault that she couldn't catch an earlier flight, despite the fact that it was already full of prepaid passengers. As she stormed away, she threatened to sue the airline.

How many times in any given day do you meet a turkey? Some people do, in fact, seem to go out of their way to be difficult, demanding, conflict-oriented, hostile, or even obnoxious. How many seem to be such poor listeners that you wonder if you're being heard at all? I even heard of a man who seems to get some sort of thrill out of threatening people with frivolous lawsuits.

Because of our sometimes aggressive, competitive, or impatient nature, this subject seems particularly relevant to men. I believe that in order to live a truly joyful and fulfilling life, we must learn to respond to turkeys in a whole new way. After all, if we wait for the most difficult segment of society to change their ways, I'm afraid we're in for a very long wait.

Rather than feeling frustrated, disappointed, hopeless, and stressed-out simply because there are jerks in our world, we can instead learn to look the other way; to ignore them. The key, I believe, lies in stepping back and seeing how much attention a turkey tends to demand, and how that attention pulls you away from everything else that is going on—all the good, ethical stuff. It's actually quite fascinating.

You deal with dozens, maybe even hundreds of people each day. At least 95 percent of them are relatively polite, kind, and competent. Most people don't shove you, nor do they cut in front of you. Neither do most people interrupt you or flip you off. On the freeway, there are tens of thousands of drivers. There are a few aggressive bad apples, but a vast majority are just fine. In fact, I've asked many audiences the following question: If you have twenty things to do in a day and nineteen of them go well—which one do you talk about over dinner? Most people admit they'll talk about the one thing that went wrong. A similar question can be asked about people. If you deal with twenty people, and nineteen of them are normal, well-intended, relatively nice people, but one of them is a real jerk—which one is the subject of conversation?

Because the turkeys are by definition obnoxious, they will tend to steal your attention—they will pull you away from and encourage you to lose sight of everyone else, the 90 or even 95 percent of people who are nice, thoughtful, competent, and fair.

What seems to work like magic is to respond to turkeys as if they were the abnormality that they are. Don't give them the time of day—don't give them your valuable attention, your time, or even a second thought. By all means, don't give away your power to them. Turkeys thrive and feed on attention. So, when you see a turkey being himself, instead of feeding him with your attention, instead simply brush it off as one more jerk who is the exception, rather than the rule.

As simple as this sounds, it really works. Each time you see a turkey, rather than turning it into a big deal, thereby exacerbating the irritation you feel, it will become instead a reminder that most people aren't, in fact, turkeys. What a great way to turn a negative into a positive.

The result will be that, instead of being bummed out or angry when you see people being turkeys, you'll actually be reminded, instead, of how normal, kind and together most people really are. The turkey will be the source of comparison—nothing more, nothing less.

Who would have thought that a turkey could actually be a good thing—a reminder that most people aren't like them? So, even when someone is obnoxious, even if it seems like it's on purpose, don't let it bug you—don't let the "turkeys" get you down!

31

RID YOURSELF OF A BUSY MIND

It's always tough to get rid of a bad habit. It's especially hard, however, when that habit is not only socially acceptable, but actually admired. This is why it's so tough to escape the grips of a busy mind. It's a real problem, but isn't usually thought of as such.

On the surface, it could seem like a busy mind would be advantageous. After all, a person with a busy mind could have a lot of balls in the air, think of ten things at once, get a lot done, and all of that. Yet, on a deeper level, a busy mind creates all sorts of problems—agitation, stress, and worry, to name a few.

A quiet mind is calm. It's from this still place that creative thoughts and ideas have a chance to percolate, to pop up as if out of the blue. A quiet mind is peaceful, happy, responsive, and extremely efficient. How many times have you had a brilliant idea or had a solution come to you when you least expected it? How often have you remembered something only after you had given up and stopped thinking about it? Far from being lazy, a quiet mind is brilliant and on target, virtually all of the time.

When the mind is overly busy, however, the reverse is true. A busy mind is the breeding ground for agitation and a sense of hurry. It's habitual, ineffective, and prone to mistakes. When the mind is too filled up, it's easy to sweat the small stuff, even the tiny stuff. Like a sprinter on the starting line, you're always just a moment away from exploding, always on edge. How many times have you overreacted when you had too much on your mind?

Think of a beehive, absolutely filled to the brim, bursting at the seams with busy bees. Now imagine that ten more are trying to squeeze inside. There's no space, and the crowded bees become increasingly irritated. That's the nature of a busy mind—too many thoughts going on at once, all clamoring for your attention. It's as if each thought is yelling out, "Think of me, think of me!" The mind is so filled to capacity that every little added thing, no matter how small, is seen as a burden. Something minor goes wrong, but it seems huge. Your wife or girlfriend says the wrong thing, but you take it personally. There is a glitch at work; you panic and it seems like a big deal. There's no room for error. It's simply too crowded in there.

Of course, there are many times when you absolutely must actively use your mind, times when it's in your best interest—it's the only way to go. For example, when you're trying to figure something out or think through a problem that requires your intellect. Or when you're planning, comparing, remembering, or calculating. These times and others require an active mind.

You'll be surprised, however, at how often it's unnecessary to have a head full of thoughts, and how advantageous it is instead to allow your mind to become free and clear. Just as dust settling allows us to see more clearly, so too does a settled mind. By making the conscious decision to keep fewer thoughts active at any given time, you allow a different kind of intelligence to take over—one that doesn't require as much effort. You might call it wisdom.

This is one of those things that, once you've experienced it, you'll be convinced of its value. And luckily, it's simple to implement. All you need to do is pay attention—be aware—of what's going on in your mind at any given time. Begin practicing during times when it's just you and your thoughts; while driving, for example, or exercising or in between meetings. Simply allow your mind to settle, to be calm.

Right away, you'll notice yourself feeling less stressed. You'll also notice that an appropriate, often brilliant, flow of thoughts will emerge as needed. You won't have to do anything—it will just happen. As time goes on and your confidence in this process is increased, you'll find yourself spending more time in a calm state of mind and less time worried and stressed. By ridding yourself of a busy mind, you'll create a happier and wiser you.

32

CREATE AN "EASIER LIFE" LIST

Oh no, not another list to create! Don't worry, no cause for alarm. I assure you this one's different. An easier life list is not another to-do list. Most lists are simply reminders of things you have to do. They help you prioritize, keep track of things, and remember appointments. They can certainly be helpful, but they can, at times, make you feel overwhelmed as well. When we rely on lists, we're constantly being reminded of all we have to do. Although they're necessary, they do tend to reinforce the problem.

Creating an easier life list is a simple method of identifying ways to make your life simpler, easier, and better. The purpose of creating such a list is to give you concrete, quantifiable ways to take away pressure or give you more time. In order to qualify for the list, the idea, if implemented, would in some way reduce the stress in your life. Along with the list itself, it's also helpful to include an explanatory sentence or two to reinforce the reason(s) why the idea is such a good idea.

Here's an example of what your partial list might look like.

1. *Hire a housecleaner.* This would make my life simpler because I'd have more time to do things other than cleaning.

2. *Hire a gardener.* I spend most of my weekends mowing the lawn and taking care of the yard. By having someone else do these things, I'd have more time to enjoy myself. I'd rather work an extra few hours at the office doing what I do best and leave the gardening to someone who does it better than me.

3. *Move to a smaller house or apartment.* I'm sick of the bills, the maintenance, the cleaning. I'd like to have less to take care of and less to spend money on.

4. *Quit a committee.* I have too many responsibilities and too little time. Something has to give. By this time next month, I'm going to quit at least one nonessential committee or commitment.

5. *Practice saying no.* I'm in the habit of saying yes too often, even to things I don't really want to do. I'm going to start saying no so I can stop compounding the problem.

Obviously, these are just a few of the many items that could be on the list. By creating the list, you are planting the seeds in your mind and are far more likely to follow through either now, or at some time in the future.

Again, notice how the items on the list are limited to those things that would clearly make your life easier. It's quite interesting and effective to create one of these lists because, once you do, it's pretty difficult to justify to yourself not putting the idea into practice. For example, suppose the above list was yours and it was sitting by your telephone. The next time someone called you to do something that you didn't have time for and didn't really want to do, you'd think twice before agreeing. If you had no such list, you might impulsively say yes, simply out of habit.

Recently, a man who traveled a great deal for business told me that he had created an easier life list and had included the idea, "Never agree to a trip when you have the option not to go." He said he was shocked at how often he did actually have a choice in the matter. He told me he still travels more than he would like, but he has cut almost 20 percent off the top. He said he never would have made such enormous strides had he not taken the time to think about and write down, specifically, what would make his life easier.

Another man told me that he had hired a tutor to help his two sons with their homework. Again, this stemmed from one of these lists. He said that he had always thought of having a tutor as eccentric. However, he realized that the tutor could teach his sons in an hour what would take him five or six.

Everyone's list is going to be different because everyone's strengths, weaknesses, financial situation, and preferences are unique. I hope you'll consider creating one of these lists for yourself, because I think you'll be pleasantly surprised at how much difference it can make when it's in writing, right there in front of you.

33

KEEP IN MIND THAT
THE FANTASY IS OFTEN BETTER
THAN THE REALITY

On the surface, this could seem like a negative suggestion. After all, why would you want to assume that something wouldn't be as great as you imagined it would be? That's a legitimate question, particularly when the suggestion is coming from an optimist. Let me ease your mind—there is a really good answer! In fact, keeping this thought fresh in your mind can save you a tremendous amount of grief and stress.

I'll start off with a dramatic example. Over the years, I've spoken to numerous men who have had affairs. They met someone really special and, of course, imagined how exciting and fulfilling such a relationship would be. Certainly, they rationalized to themselves, "Starting up an intimate relationship with this woman will fill some void in my life."

That was the fantasy.

The reality, of course, was quite different. Invariably, things didn't work out so well. There were hurt feelings, ruined marriages, and destroyed families. The person who started out seeming so wonderful turned out to be all too human. The excitement wore off, but the stress and pain continued. They were worried about covering their tracks, getting caught, and explaining themselves. Their thoughts, worries, and guilt haunted them, often well after the affair was over.

There are many less dramatic examples of the same reality. Here's a personal example. For as long as I can remember, I've always wanted to own a boat. Keeping this idea in mind, however, has kept me from acting on my desire. The fantasy I have is that I'd be zipping around beautiful lakes pulling my kids on water skis. And it's possible I would do some of that.

The far more likely reality, of course, is that the boat would sit in my carport fifty-one weeks a year or more. The truth is, I know close to nothing about boats, electronics, or how to maintain such an expensive toy. Most likely, a boat would be one more thing to try to find time to use and one more thing to insure, maintain, and take care of. I have several close friends who have boats, but none of them use the boats, at least not very often. The closest beautiful lake to our home is about a four-hour drive.

Many expensive items fall into the same category. Many people dream of a vacation home. The fantasy is wonderful. However, the reality, for most people, is that they simply don't use it very much. Plus, the expense and maintenance creates a great deal of stress and hassle. There are other unanticipated issues, as well. Now that you own the place, will you ever go anywhere else? Or how about when Aunt Margaret wants to use it—what will you say? It goes on and on.

Some vacations are like that, too. I met a man who dreamed of owning a motor home. He fantasized about how much fun it would be to pack up the family and drive across the country. But after his first experience with all six of his family members in such a small space—complete with fighting, lack of privacy, babies crying all night, and other things—he very humbly wished that he had never bought it. He realized that the fantasy was great, but the reality was something quite different.

This strategy isn't meant to be a dream-crusher, nor is it meant to be negative. It's simply a reality check. For some people, a boat or a vacation home, or an expensive new car is the greatest thing in the world. My neighbor, for example, loves his motor home and my in-laws love theirs. Everyone's different, but most of us could benefit from knowing the difference between fantasy and reality, in at least some areas of our lives.

Keeping in mind that the fantasy of something is often better than the real thing is helpful because it keeps you from longing for things. When you know that many things aren't quite what they seem, you're able to be more easily satisfied with what you have. Keeping this statement in mind will encourage you to ask yourself some important questions before you act impulsively. You'll also be less disappointed when you can't have something you want. A man I met was a bit disappointed when he couldn't afford the car he really wanted. But when he realized that the fantasy was probably quite a bit better than the reality—for example, the payments, upkeep and higher insurance costs—he saw it quite differently. Instead of feeling bad, he was relieved.

This strategy doesn't suggest that it's a bad idea to fantasize about things—only that it's a good idea to realize that what you think you want may not turn out to be quite the dream you imagined it to be. Knowing this can save you from a ton of stress and will help you enjoy the life you already have.

34

READ YOUR AUDIENCE

One of the keys to being an effective public speaker is to be able to read your audience. In a nutshell, this means that if your audience is receptive to what you're saying, you continue on the same track; if not, you make adjustments. You're constantly checking in with the people you're speaking to—making sure your message is being accepted in the manner in which it is intended. Reading your audience also enables you to know when it's time to repeat a major point you are making, as well as when it's time to quit.

The implications to being able to read your audience go far beyond public speaking. In fact, it can be argued that your audience is everyone you have a relationship with, or, for that matter, everyone you come into contact with.

Don't you agree that one of the most irritating things to deal with is when someone is talking, not so much with, but at you? And although you're bored stiff, totally disinterested in what the person is saying, and you don't have time to listen anyway, the person just keeps on talking. Despite your subtle clues—wandering eyes, glancing at your watch, and yawning—he keeps right on going.

As hard as it is to admit, there are probably times when you and I are the ones who aren't reading our audience very well; times when we're talking—but the person we're talking to wishes we would stop. And although being aware of this problem doesn't guarantee it will never happen, it sure reduces the likelihood and makes it easier to recover. There's no specific technique to memorize here or any particular way to go about reading your audience. Awareness is the key. When you're talking to someone, simply pay attention to the person's body language; check in with their level of interest. Be aware of their questions—or lack thereof. If you find they aren't interested, don't take it personally. Simply find an appropriate way to bring the conversation to an end.

This is a polite, respectful, and easy way to enhance your relationships with people. By minimizing the amount of time we force people to listen to us and being aware of their relative receptivity to what we are saying, we also become more in tune with those times when that same person is "with us" or interested in what we are saying. That's what connection is all about—taking advantage of those times when both people are in synch and not being overly concerned when you're not.

This same idea can be used while on the telephone, in a slightly different way. When you call someone, try asking the simple question, "Is this a good time for you?" If so, great! If it's not, make that okay with you, too. Either way, you both win. Unless what you have to say is an emergency, you're probably both better off postponing a conversation if the time isn't right. I've had so many people thank me for asking them this question. Many times, I've been told that I was the first person to do so. So often, someone you're calling is preoccupied, running out the door, or in the middle of something. They pick up the phone without really thinking about whether or not they have time to talk. By letting them off the hook, you become their hero. Can you imagine how relieved you'd be if the tables were turned? You'd be thrilled and grateful—and so will they.

You don't have to be a public speaker to take advantage of the wisdom of reading your audience. Anyone can do it—and it really works.

35

HAVE CONFLICT WITHOUT
IT HAVING YOU

I'm not certain, but I doubt that even the Dalai Lama would suggest that there will ever come a time when there will be no conflict
that we must deal with in our lives. Yet, there's a tremendous difference
between having conflict, and it having you. In other words, while we will
often have to negotiate, settle for less, do without, or simply not get what
we want, that doesn't mean we have to become immobilized, stressed, or
despondent because of it. There's a big difference between having a preference for something—even a strong one—and being attached to an outcome.

The simple truth of the matter is that there will be times when, if I
get what I want, it means you don't get what you want, or vice versa. I
might desire to paint the house white, while Kris insists it should be green.
Unfortunately, there's only one house. There are so many conflicting interests in life that it's impossible to always get what we want. What's good
in one sense is bad in another. There was a heat wave this past summer
in California. There were a number of energy alerts, suggesting a threat
to guaranteed air conditioning. One group of people was insisting that
the state needed to build additional power stations. Another argued that
we have too many already and that to add more would be harmful to the

environment. One thing is certain: We won't be both building power plants *and* not building them. There is a conflict of interest.

Part of the solution is to become less surprised when conflict arises, therefore taking it less personally. Rather than saying to yourself, "That's not fair," try thinking this instead: "Of course there's conflict here—that's no big surprise." When you depersonalize the conflict, you'll be amazed at how much less you'll be gripped by it. You'll be able to take a step back and see the bigger picture. You'll be more able to see both sides of the story and to admit that peaceful living involves some give and take. Somehow, acknowledging this to ourselves helps us to resolve our conflicts and to stop sweating the small stuff.

I was at a shopping mall when I observed two men arguing over one parking place. They were both really mad, yelling and screaming at each other, each insisting that he, not the other, was entitled to that particular spot. When I finished my shopping and headed back toward my car, they were still standing there arguing. Unbelievably, there were plenty of spots less than a hundred yards away. Had either one of them had the wisdom to understand the nature of conflict, the entire situation would have been resolved before it even started.

I learned a great deal from a friend of mine who was engaged in a high-stakes negotiation. I was amazed at his ability to be tough, yet at the same time detached from the ultimate outcome. It wasn't that he didn't care—he cared passionately. It wasn't that he didn't need the money—he did. Instead, what he realized and shared with me was that conflict was inherent, almost assured in this type of deal, and that one simply needed to make allowances for this fact. Obviously, both sides want the best deal possible, and both are entitled to give it their best shot.

"Where's the emergency?" he asked. He added, "There's no need to panic." I saw his point and have attempted, ever since, to extend his wisdom to other areas in my life. And it's not as difficult as I imagined it would be.

Making peace with conflict doesn't mean you don't ever fight for what you want or what you believe in. It does, however, suggest you're a bit more selective about what you choose to fight about. Ironically, however, when you learn to have conflict—without it having you—you'll end up getting your way, even more than before. Because you'll have a more open, receptive mind, you'll see solutions where others see only problems. Furthermore, because you'll come across as less adversarial, others will be more open to your point of view. You'll discover new ways to resolve your conflicts, all the while maintaining your peace of mind.

36

TAKE THE QUIRKS WITH
THE PERKS

A while back, I started an informal experiment. As I traveled around the country, I kept track of the types of conversations I was having with men—what we talked about and what the focus was on.

It was interesting to me because, while virtually everyone let me know, in no uncertain terms, what the quirks of their careers, wives, girlfriends, and other parts of their lives were, it was a rare person who focused instead on the perks of their lives. In fact, most never mentioned them at all.

For example, a gentleman in New York complained that he had to be at work by 7:00 A.M., but I had to question him to find out that he was off by 4:00. Someone in Ohio would become visibly upset when he spoke of how his boss had a neurotic need to fill each day with at least one short, but nonetheless unnecessary and boring meeting. Then, I'd find out from someone else that this same boss encouraged family time and extra vacations, which was somewhat rare in his industry. Others would complain about the incredible stress of the job, but would neglect to mention the on-site gym, casual Fridays, or the fact that they were paid quite a bit more than others doing similar jobs for other firms.

I would never suggest that any job didn't include some stress, plenty of hassles, trade-offs, and things to complain about. I would suggest, however, that most jobs have at least some really nice perks that accompany the quirks. The question is, why do we so often zero in on the hassles and the parts that are less than perfect, and completely take for granted the parts of our jobs—and lives—that are really quite nice? The simple truth is, life is full of trade-offs.

I overheard a man expressing to his friend his dissatisfaction about the fact that his wife didn't earn income outside the home. A few moments later, I discovered that his wife was home-schooling his four children. At times, it gets bizarre. For whatever reason, many of us are tempted to act as though it's actually possible, and that we are somehow entitled, to "have it all." We want jobs with no hassles, relationships that are perfect, kids who are great athletes and straight-A students. We want to be in huge demand, yet we resent it when the phone rings. We want an interesting career, but we don't want to have to travel very often. And so forth.

I always chuckle when famous people, who thrive upon attention from the public and the media, turn around and complain about the attention they receive and their lack of privacy. They so desperately want and are willing to accept the perks—all of them—but complain about the quirks that go with the territory. It seems to me that we can all learn from a similar pattern that exists in our own lives.

Lately, I've been gently reminding myself to "take the quirks with the perks," and it's been very helpful. When I find myself complaining about my day, I remind myself that, along with the parts of the day that may have been less than perfect, there was plenty to be happy about too.

One day, when I came home, I launched into a detailed description of an uncomfortable conference call I had been involved in. Kris, who is too wise to get sucked in very often, smiled at me and said, "Gee, that's too bad. Didn't you also have lunch today with a good friend that you hadn't seen in a while?" Indeed I had. And it was good for me to hear that from Kris. Of all the joyful things to do in life, certainly one of most enjoyable is to meet up with old friends. The truth was, I had had a wonderful day. But my knee-jerk reaction was to relive the one negative experience instead of the gift I had been given.

I'm not suggesting, even for a moment, that we put on a fake smile and pretend that our lives are wonderful or that we appreciate the hassles of our day. Not at all. I'm simply pointing out that by focusing only on that which is wrong, we rob ourselves of the quality of life that we are capable of having. Fooling ourselves works in both directions. Just as some people pretend everything is wonderful when it's not, others act as though everything is terrible, when that's not really the case.

It's a simple idea, but it really does help to put problems and hassles into perspective. When you remember to accept the quirks that come with the perks, life will seem less stressful, right away.

37

FIND A PLACE TO PARK

I once heard Wayne Dyer suggest that many people drive around "looking for no place to park." I had to laugh because the same day I heard him suggest this, I was in a car with a man who was complaining that there was no place to park.

The suggestion, of course, is that what you're looking for is a parking place—but sometimes, all you notice are all the places you can't park. You notice the filled spaces, the lack of parking, and the crowds, forgetting that all you need is one free space. Instead of focusing our attention on the one thing we need and patiently waiting for it, we zero in on everything else. Then, when we finally do find a place to park, rather than feeling grateful, we complain that it took too long. How can you ever feel satisfied or happy with that type of mentality? You can't—and you won't.

Somewhere in the midst of all those cars is the one space that is waiting for you—and the one and only space that you need. You don't need lots of places to park; you only need one. When you keep this in mind, it takes much of the frustration away from the search. Instead of reminding yourself of and obsessing over the shortage of parking, you calmly drive around with a watchful eye, looking for an opening. And when you eventually find one, whether it's in three minutes or thirteen, you park the car and get out.

This simple shift in attitude can extend to many aspects of life other than parking. How often, for example, do we stomp around, frustrated because "there are no good opportunities out there?" Just yesterday, I heard two people say those exact words with regard to the Internet. Yet, today in the newspaper, there were stories suggesting the opposite.

We complain that there are no honest people anymore—or that it's nearly impossible to find "good help." Or we're upset that it's too crowded in certain locations or that our kids' school is no good.

The truth is, we're almost always going to find what we're looking for. If our attention is zeroed in on the shortcomings of a hotel, we will certainly find plenty to complain about. If we're looking for something to be critical of—in another person, in our way of life, in where we live, or what we do for a living—we will absolutely, positively find plenty of things that are less than perfect. As men, we can be experts in finding flaws, poking holes in arguments, or seeing imperfections, if that's what we want to do. I guarantee you that if your goal was to find fault with this book, you'd hate it.

On the other hand, the same logic works in reverse. For the most part, if your goal is to look for what's right—whether that means finding the perfect parking place, the right job or neighborhood or school for your kids, or people to spend time with, or a place to go on vacation—then that's what you'll find. You'll simply sort through all the factors and choices, eliminate the ones that aren't right for you or that don't suit your needs, and you'll zero in on the perfect match. It's really that simple.

I once spoke to a man who was about to give up his profession because he couldn't handle the rejection that it entailed. However, while we spoke, he realized that he was focusing only on the number of rejections, instead of the fact that eventually he did make some sales. Once a sale was made, the number of rejections it took to get there became irrelevant. He started looking at his career very differently. The rejections stopped bothering him so much, which, of course, not only made him less frustrated, but turned him into a better salesperson, as well.

I challenge you to make this shift in your attitude, starting today. Instead of noticing that there's no place to park, keep your eyes open, be patient, and search for the one spot you need. Instead of noticing all the things that drive you nuts, search for what you like. Rather than focus on all the people who irritate you, allow them to drift into the background of your attention and find a few people who do meet your expectations. And when you do, say to yourself, "See, there are people out there who are okay." It's all a matter of where you direct your attention. Do you focus on the hundreds of irritants in the world because they are there— or do you focus instead on the small percentage of life that suits you?

By making this simple shift in attitude, you're going to change the way you feel about many aspects of life. Who would have thought that the way you search for a parking spot could be so important?

38

AVOID THE PURSUIT TRAP

There's no question that men are usually in pursuit of something: money, accomplishments, goals, possessions, achievements, dreams, a partner, whatever. In fact, it's hard to quantify, but I'd guess that 99 percent of our life is spent pursuing something. We work, struggle, sacrifice, climb toward and chase things—then we achieve them or not, and start again.

In terms of our personal happiness, the problem isn't the pursuit itself, but the way we tend to approach it. Without even knowing it, we often convince ourselves that we'll be satisfied when, and only when, the pursuit is complete. In other words, we've already decided that we're not going to be happy now—there's no time for that. Later, when we've done what we've set out to do, we'll be all smiles.

Unfortunately, there's a serious flaw in this way of thinking. In fact, it's an outright setup, a prescription for lifelong frustration and unhappiness. Because such a high percentage of our time is spent in the pursuit of goals, we must find a way to enjoy the actual day-to-day, moment-to-moment process of life, instead of waiting for the destination or end result. When this shift occurs, we will experience not only the satisfaction that comes from a goal successfully completed, but a thousand joys along the way. It's an entirely different way of approaching life and is ultimately more effective, too. Rather than being constantly stressed from assessing your progress toward your goal, you'll find yourself engaged and enthused each step of the way.

I was once working on a project that I figured would take approximately six months to complete. About four months into it, I became a bit impatient and started looking forward to the end. I found myself thinking (frequently), "Only two months to go," "Only seven more weeks," and so forth. In the midst of one of these thoughts, it struck me as funny what I was doing to myself. I was going to spend the next two months working on the project, no matter what. Without even knowing it, I was making the decision that I wasn't going to enjoy it, but rather, I was just going to get through it, *then* I'd be happy. How absurd and foolish. I thought to myself, "Wait a minute. This is my life. Why not instead make the best of and enjoy the moments between now and then?" It was a simple insight, but it made all the difference in my experience. I still looked forward to the completion of the work, but I was also able to enjoy the fifty or sixty days in the meantime.

I've learned that the process of life—including the work, the obstacles, even the hassles—are my life. Life isn't the end result—it's everything in between the beginning and the end. It includes the difficult conversations, a simple act of kindness, walking the dog, watching a sunset, helping your child with homework, washing dishes, driving to work. It's day-to-day living.

On the surface, this seems rather obvious, yet it's not easy. Our minds are so goal-oriented, we fool ourselves into thinking, "I'll enjoy myself later when I get through this mess." We forget that "the mess" itself is the essence of life. Indeed, there will always be conflict to deal with, unfinished business, and unreturned phone calls. There will always be projects we are working on, bills to pay, and fires to put out. There will usually be someone mad at us for something and plenty of things to do. That's just life.

So keep on pursuing—that seems to be part of being a man. But keep in mind, too, that the bulk of your life is spent, not at the finish line, but in the race itself. This simple shift in perspective can enhance your life in many ways. Rather than continuing to postpone your enjoyment, you can start right now.

39

THINK C-A-L-M

What do you envision when you think of the word "calm"? To me, it represents a peaceful state of mind. A calm mind is extremely effective because it's not easily distracted. It's resilient and is able to see right to the heart of the matter. It's reassuring to be around someone who has a calm mind because they exude a sense of quiet confidence. Someone who remains calm in the midst of turmoil doesn't sweat the small stuff.

To use the word "calm" as an acronym can be a powerful tool. Doing so can remind you of your goal to become a calmer person, and can reinforce to you the many benefits of being calmer.

The letter C can stand for "centered." A calm person is very centered. He is able to be with someone without having his mind elsewhere. This is very nourishing to both himself and to the person he is with. This quality makes it easy for him to have great relationships.

The letter A stands for "alive and attentive." A calm person can be touched by life. He feels the joy of being alive. When you are calm, boredom is nonexistent. Life is fun again.

The letter L stands for "lighthearted." A calm person doesn't take himself or anyone else too seriously. He has a great sense of humor. He can laugh at his own humanity, and forgives himself when he makes mistakes. A calm person doesn't see life as an emergency!

Finally, the letter M stands for "magical." Life as seen through the eyes of a calm person appears to be magical. It's a gift that is cherished and treasured each and every day. A calm person doesn't take his life for granted. He stops to smell the roses and to take in the beauty around him. He reflects, often, about the mystery of life and how glad he is to be here.

Jot down "C-A-L-M" on a piece of paper and toss it into your brief-case. Or, put it on your desk or on the refrigerator. Then, each time you see it, you'll get a subtle reminder to do your best to stay calm. The more you reinforce and prioritize this idea, the easier it will be to become the way you look at life. I think you'll enjoy being calm—good luck!

40

ELIMINATE ENTITLEMENT
THINKING

I'm convinced that one of the keys to being a satisfied person is to eliminate, as much as possible, something that I call entitlement thinking. This is also a surefire way to reduce stress and to make a better impression on others.

Entitlement thinking means that you believe you deserve and are entitled to certain things—someone else's attention, perfect service, the finest products, or anything else. There is a noticeable lack of humility. Instead, you adopt an air of arrogance.

Occasionally, when I talk about this issue, someone is confused and says, "Are you saying I don't deserve great service if I'm paying for it?" The answer to that question is no. What I'm talking about is a step beyond that. Entitlement is an attitude that suggests, "This is my right," "I'm special," and "I can't possibly tolerate anything less."

If you reflect on it, entitlement thinking is the opposite of gratitude thinking. When someone is appreciative of something, it's almost as if they are surprised at how wonderful everything is. It's refreshing to be around them. When there is good service, they say thanks and they're happy. If someone listens to them, they are enthused and grateful. Even if they're used to having nice things, there is a sense that they know how fortunate they are. It's in their attitude. If someone falls short of perfection, they make allowances in their mind and in their heart. They give people a break. They are happy because they are able to seek excellence, yet still keep their perspective about things. They don't sweat the small stuff.

People with an entitlement attitude, on the other hand, expect things to be perfect and sweat everything. They demand perfection and can't understand why the people aren't asking, "How high?" when they say "Jump." Moreover, they are annoyed and bothered when things aren't perfect. They can become abusive without even knowing it, because their sense of entitlement is so ingrained.

Entitlement thinking shows up in relationships, as well. Someone will say, "Wait a minute. You've always been there for me," as if the fact that someone has been with them in the past entitles them to that person's company for a lifetime. That's different from commitment, which says, "Sure we're committed to each other, but I know I need (and want) to remember to appreciate you. I never want to take you for granted!"

A good example of entitlement thinking shows up in very spoiled children. I overheard a boy say to his mom, "Mom, take me to the mall." It wasn't a request; it was a command. It was obvious that he felt entitled. He felt that his mother was there to serve him. It was ugly, disrespectful, and wrong.

Another place you see entitlement thinking pop up is with some famous or very wealthy people. Someone has been blessed with extreme talent, timing, and good fortune, but they lose sight of the good fortune part of that equation. It's so refreshing to see a famous person who's humble; this shows that he or she remembers to be grateful for the fact that things have fallen into place so well. When someone lacks all sense of humility and gets too used to being a star, it's a turnoff to be around them.

The lesson for the rest of us is pretty obvious. It's a gift to be human and to have any degree of privilege. All that's necessary to avoid entitlement thinking is to remember that. Be grateful. Don't take things for granted. You can prefer and even demand excellence without becoming obnoxious about it. In fact, if you can keep that balance between wanting excellence, preferring it, and working toward it—without being obsessed by it—you'll be on your way to a perfectly balanced and happier life.

41

LEARN FROM FELLOW

"SWEAT"-ERS

Not too long ago, someone asked me how I learned to stop sweating the small stuff. I had to laugh when I shared with him that one of the ways was by trying to learn from others who were too uptight or stressed. Indeed, when you see how ineffective it is, and how badly it looks when someone is overreactive about little things, it's easy to remind yourself that that's not the way you want to be.

Not long ago, Kris and I went jogging with our dog, Ty. He is a very well behaved golden retriever, about as friendly as a dog can be. We had just begun our jog when I saw a few people up the path, maybe a quarter of a mile ahead. I reached over and put Ty's leash on him to be absolutely sure he wouldn't bother them.

As we jogged by the two women walkers, we both smiled and said hello, Ty calmly at our side on his leash. At that moment, one of them glared at us and said under her breath in a nasty, harsh tone of voice, "I see you know about the leash rule. I just saw you put it on your dog." In all seriousness, at first I thought she was kidding. How anyone could get uptight around Ty is beyond me—but being visibly upset about a leash that was on a dog, just not early enough, was almost too strange to believe. She was so tense about it that it was obvious that she felt this was really big stuff.

As always, however, when someone gets bent out of shape over something really small, something good came out of it. It reminded Kris and me how easy it is to lose perspective and to turn something really small into something far more significant. The truth is, all of us—myself included—are capable of getting too uptight and sweating the small stuff.

The next time someone sweats the small stuff big time, try something a little different. Rather than feeling bothered by someone who is acting bothered, see if you can use the situation to remind yourself of how you want to learn to respond to life. Use other people's overreactions as a way to learn, and you'll have an unlimited number of opportunities to practice patience and healthy responses.

Whether you observe someone yelling at a waitress or sales clerk, flipping out over a parking space dispute, overreacting in public, or screaming about poor service, try to see it in a different light. Instead of thinking poorly about that person or bringing it up critically to others as a form of entertainment (as I have just done!), choose instead to take note of the overreaction and how out-of-perspective the response to the situation was.

When you do this, it really helps smooth your own reactions to life. The next time you feel yourself getting upset over some little thing, it will be a bit easier for you to take it in stride. Who knows? Perhaps the next time you're walking by someone with a dog, you'll be able to refrain from bawling them out.

42

BE FOR SOMETHING
RATHER THAN AGAINST IT

It's amazing to me how you can take an essentially identical position or goal, and, depending on how you characterize it in your mind, you can create either hopefulness and peace of mind or stress and angst. Here's what I mean.

Suppose you are against war—and who isn't? When you are against something, however, it can often suggest a subtle conflict within yourself. Often, you are taking an aggressive stance against that which you believe is wrong and destructive. When the subject comes up, you protest. You become animated, perhaps even angry. I remember a conversation I was having with some people, years ago in college. One of the guys yelled out, "I hate the government and the arms race!" He was visibly upset and agitated. I believe his actual intention was positive, yet the way he was expressing it and thinking about it created enormous stress for himself. I actually thought he was going to have a heart attack. A good question to ask might be this: How can hatred lead to peace?

On the other hand, you could just as easily decide that you were for peace. You could be an advocate for peace, live a peaceful life, and choose to be a role model. You could work for peaceful causes and become part of the solution. The Dalai Lama, the winner of the 1989 Nobel Peace Prize, is very much for peace—but he would be hard-pressed to raise his voice. Mother Teresa certainly did a great deal to promote peace in her lifetime, as well. Yet, she did so without creating grief for herself and those around her.

Obviously, most of us will never reach this level of inner peace, but it's easy to see the distinction. You can see how easy it is to be working with very positive intentions, yet still find a way to drive yourself nuts. Some environmental activists, for example, are doing great things— choosing to be vegetarians, picking up litter, cleaning up the beaches, planting trees, recycling, and raising awareness as well as money for the causes they believe in. Others, however, yell and scream, block traffic, chain themselves to trees, and starve themselves in an attempt to accomplish their goals.

The same choice exists in relation to far more mundane subjects. You could, for example, be in favor of simplicity, as I am. You could make choices that promote a simpler life, that indicate your preference for free time and open space. You could decide that more isn't always better. Instead of overscheduling your life, you could attempt to prevent being overwhelmed by living at a sane pace. Yet instead of this position, you could be against clutter and chaos. In this case, clutter might drive you crazy. You would feel as if you were fighting an endless battle. Everything from phone calls to the daily mail would frustrate you. You would wince at your overcrowded schedule, yet you would probably not do much about it. Rather than leave a little early for work, anticipating traffic and maybe listen to some quiet music in the car, you'd be more likely to wait until the last minute, rush out the door, and be frustrated at all the traffic.

It's an interesting subject to think about. It can seem, on the surface, like this idea is nothing more than splitting hairs, and it's easy to think,

What difference could it make? Yet, when you play around with it, you'll notice an enormous difference in the way you feel, depending on how you choose to characterize the things you care about.

So whether it has to do with personal, ethical, or work-related issues—regardless of how passionate you may be about them—experiment with looking at issues two ways: "for" and "against." My guess is that, most of the time, you'll be less stressed and happier when you choose to be for something rather than against it. And you may be surprised at how much more effective you'll be, as well.

43

BLOW OFF STEAM

One of the tendencies many men have is to allow things to fester, to build up, and accumulate before we deal with it. Then, out of the blue, we explode! An easy way to prevent this from happening is to find healthy ways to blow off steam.

A man shared with me how frustrated he was with a coworker who mispronounced his name. Apparently, he had done so hundreds of times over several years. The man said it was driving him crazy. He admitted to me, however, that he had never brought it up. For whatever reasons, he thought the man would eventually get it right. Blowing off steam in this instance would have been to address the issue right away, before it had a chance to get blown out of proportion. In all likelihood, a friendly correction would have solved the problem.

This example is symbolic of so many things that start out small, build over time, and end up stressing us out. Whether it's a habit one of your kids has developed that is starting to bother you or the habit of your spouse, parents, or a friend, it's a good idea in many instances to share your frustration in a healthy, honest way.

You might think to yourself, "It's my issue, why bring it up?" That's a great question, and if you're asking it, you're right—it is your issue. Yet you can make it perfectly clear that you're aware that something is your issue—and still bring it up. By getting it off your chest and being honest, you're doing several things. First, if someone is making an honest mistake, as in the person mispronouncing his colleague's name, you give him a chance to correct himself. Second, in many instances, the simple act of sharing your frustration in a nondefensive manner clears the air and allows you to let go of it altogether. In other words, it ceases to bother you.

Here's a personal example. I was working with someone whom I believed was coming across a bit too harshly to others. As much as I tried to let it go, it continued to bother me. I felt it was a poor reflection on my own relationship with those people. It was building up in my mind to the point of frustration. Finally, I decided to let off some steam. We had a conversation about my perceptions, which cleared the air immediately. What I realized was that, had I cleared the air sooner, I would have minimized, if not eliminated, most of my frustration about this issue.

Blowing off steam can take other forms, as well. Some people feel that a great physical workout blows off steam and reduces stress. Others, like myself, enjoy spending a little time alone or in nature. When I get away for a day, or even a few hours, it's as if any stress I have accumulated begins to fade away. Others have hobbies they love—sailing, hiking, working on cars, or reading. Still others find that having someone to talk to—a friend or even a therapist—is a tremendous help.

The key, it seems, is to blow off steam early, before it has a chance to build too much momentum. This way, you can keep small stuff small. So if exercise is your thing, do it before you're feeling stressed out—think of it as a preventive measure. The same is true however you choose to blow off steam. If you think of this as a healthy thing to do—and you do it early and often—you may be pleasantly surprised at how much less stress you have to deal with.

44

AVOID THE EXCUSE, "THAT'S THE NATURE OF THE BUSINESS"

While gathering material for this book, I asked a number of men the question, "What excuses that people use bother you the most?" At the top of many lists was the ultimate cop-out, "I can't help it—that's the nature of the business." I have to agree.

We hired some people to do a construction project. At one point, just for fun, I started keeping track of how many times this same excuse was used. Every day, for two consecutive weeks, someone uttered these meaningless words.

But it's not just contractors who use this lame excuse—it's virtually everyone: bankers, restaurant workers, travel agents, lawyers, even massage therapists. A friend told me he scheduled a massage at an upscale hotel. When the masseur showed up thirty minutes late, my friend had to cancel his appointment in order to be on time for his next commitment. Rather than simply apologizing and saying, "I'm really sorry, sir, but I'm running behind," the masseur blamed it on "the nature of the business," as if to say it was out of his control. Luckily, my friend had a sense of humor.

One of the reasons it's so important not to use this excuse is that, to begin with, no one really believes you anyway. Most people think of it as nothing more than a disrespectful, lazy cop-out. So why even try? It leaves many people distrusting your integrity as well as your competence. In most cases, your customers would much prefer an honest acceptance of the fact that you and/or your business simply made a mistake, and that you'll try harder next time. Not always, but usually, an admission puts the issue to rest, reassures your customer, and puts it behind you.

Beyond that, however, is your own sense of self-respect. By blaming a problem, miscommunication, mistake, or error on the inevitability of the business, you're accepting no responsibility. It's as if you're saying to yourself, "I have no power" or "I'm not capable enough to make things happen." An enthusiastic, fulfilled human being would have the opposite perspective. He would behave in a way that reinforced his belief that he can make things happen, that he does have some degree of control over the things he is involved with.

On a lighter note, if you are on the receiving end of this common excuse, don't sweat it. All it means is that you have run into someone who hasn't yet realized how silly it is to use it. Be compassionate and patient. Instead of being irritated, be glad it's not you using the words, "It's the nature of the business."

45

BE AWARE OF THE
"TAKEN AWAY" TRAP

I've seen this trap hurt so many people, on such a consistent basis, that I felt it had to be included in this book. There's no question in my mind that the "taken away" trap warrants some serious reflection.

Becoming aware of the predictable way in which most of us perceive that something has been taken away from us is extremely helpful. I'm not sure if it's something we're born with or something we learn, but there seems to be a universal tendency in people to respond adversely, defensively, and negatively to the feeling that something is being taken away from them. I refer to this as a trap because you're the one who is exposed to the fury and frustration that is felt when it seems that something has been taken away from you.

Perhaps the best way to explain this dynamic is to offer a comparison. Suppose, for example, that someone was hired to do a job and was offered two paid weeks off per year. Let's assume he worked two years, and each year, he happily took his two weeks. The following year, he was offered an additional paid week off. He cheerfully went off to Hawaii. That's scenario one.

Here's scenario two: The same man was hired for the same job, with the same pay, but was offered three weeks off per year. He worked for two years and enjoyed each week of his vacation. The following year, however, he was informed that, next year, he would only get two weeks of paid vacation.

How do you suppose he would react to having had a week taken away? Most likely he would feel ripped off and angry. I'm not suggesting he shouldn't feel that way, but it's really interesting if you study the facts. In the first scenario, the man had seven paid weeks off over a period of three years. He was totally satisfied. In the second scenario, however, the same man was given eight weeks off over three years, but was furious. He received more, but was ultimately disappointed.

One of the most vivid examples of this dynamic comes from a friend who shared with me a story about his housecleaner. For about a year, he paid his housecleaner almost twice the going rate, and, according to him, far more than any of her other clients paid her. When he had a downturn in his finances, he was forced to cut back on all of his expenses. He really valued her work and the help she provided.

To make a long story short, however, he told her that if he were to continue using her housecleaning services, he would have cut back her pay. Despite the fact that she was still going to make more than she was from her other clients, she became angry at him and quit. I'm not defending his decision or criticizing her response. All I'm saying is that her reaction was predictable because, to a large degree, it's universal. Rather than being angry at all her other clients who may have been underpaying her all along, her frustration was directed solely at him—because he took something away from her.

It's helpful to know of this tendency in people because it can allow you to avoid a great number of conflicts and reduce your chances of disappointing others. It makes you think about the precedents you set, the promises you make, and the probable consequences of some of your decisions.

Obviously, there are many instances when you will have to disappoint someone or take something away. That's part of life, too. It's not necessary to fear those instances or to go crazy trying to avoid them. However, it's often the case that you can make decisions, or postpone making decisions, or make a few adjustments in what you are promising someone—until you know as many facts as possible.

As a parent, this knowledge comes in really handy. Just the other day, it looked as though I was going to be able to do something special with one of my kids—but I wasn't absolutely sure. Although I couldn't wait to tell her about it, I decided to hold back until I knew all the facts. As it turned out, I'm really glad I waited. My schedule changed, and I wasn't able to participate in that special event after all. Because I didn't make the promise in the first place, I didn't have to take anything away from her. And if you have kids, you know what that's like.

You can probably sense that there are many times that being aware of this trap can be extremely helpful—with your spouse, girlfriend, employer, someone who works for you, your kids, and so forth. By being aware of how people feel when something is taken away from them, it helps you become more sensitive to the feelings of others, and it helps keep your own stress level to a minimum.

46

HAVE A BEGINNER'S MIND

Have you ever taken a class or tried something new just for fun? Have you ever become so absorbed in something that you didn't care if you were good at it or not? Or have you ever seen little children playing a game for the first time, having so much fun that it warmed your heart? If so, you've experienced or at least observed what is sometimes called beginner's mind. When you're not self-conscious about what you look like or how much skill you have, it's as if you're an open book. You're able to have fun and keep from being too serious. You absorb the experience fully and have a sharp learning curve.

The Buddhist monk Shunryu Suzuki-Roshi has said that beginner's mind means that you have the ability to respond freshly to each moment as it arises, without too much expectation. It's almost like you get out of your own way and remove your knee-jerk reactions so that you can experience something exactly as it is, in the moment, instead of projecting your own ideas, judgments, and expectations.

When you allow yourself to have a beginner's mind, all sorts of nice things begin to happen. You'll be less irritated and stressed because you won't feel so certain about things or have such rigid responses. For example, when someone does something that typically would annoy you, instead of instantly thinking to yourself, "He shouldn't be that way," you'll be more likely to let it go and not allow it to bother you. You'll also be far less self-critical. Instead of berating yourself for your sloppy golf game, you'll do the best you can and enjoy each and every shot you take. What's more, because your mind will be clear, you'll probably lower your score.

Don't confuse a beginner's mind with a lack of sophistication. The fact of the matter is that a beginner's mind is quite wise and has an intelligence all its own. It's a willingness to keep an open mind and to admit that you don't have all the answers. It doesn't mean you aren't an expert in some things or that you don't have strong, well-thought-out opinions. It only means that you're willing to see things differently, learn something new and open your mind and your heart to a lot more fun.

Typically, of course, when confronted with a problem or something we don't like, we begin a mental process that includes plenty of angst and an actively negative imagination. We play out various scenarios in our mind, imagining the struggle and all the possible outcomes. We get ourselves all worked up and stressed about things because they don't match our rigid picture of the way things are supposed to be. We spend a lot of energy rehearsing all that could or will go wrong.

On the other hand, a beginner's mind is an open and clear channel of wisdom and possibilities. By admitting that you don't, in fact, know what's going to happen, you are able to see solutions that don't appear when your mind is certain things are going to turn out for the worst. Instead of rehearsing negative outcomes, you spend your time being effective in each moment.

A man once told me that he couldn't possibly tell his wife how unhappy he had become in their marriage because he already knew what her reaction would be. After talking about it for a while, he could see the wisdom of not knowing what the response was going to be. Instead of anticipating the worst, he could simply do his best, speak from his heart, and be open to what might happen. By becoming a beginner in his relationship, he was free to experience whatever was going to happen without letting a predetermined negative outcome get in the way. To his great surprise, the conversation became the turning point in his marriage. It opened the door to a fresh start and reinforced the grace of a beginner's mind.

You don't have to be a Zen master or practice meditation to experience the benefits of a beginner's mind. All you have to do is be open to the possibility that it's in your best interest to refrain from judgment, keep an open and clear mind, and live each moment anew as if you didn't know what was going to happen next. I hope you'll give this strategy the opportunity to ease the stress in your life. It really can make an enormous difference.

47

DON'T DO IT YOURSELF

I was with a man who was complaining about the fact that he was never able to find time for himself. He told me, "I'd pay just about anything to have a day to myself."

As I often do, I began to ask a few questions. I found out that this coming weekend had been reserved to change the oil in his car and to fix a leaking toilet. Previous weekends had been spent working in the yard, painting the house, and fixing things. If his house is anything like mine, I'd guess that the next time he'd have a free day would be in about fifty years.

As I said, he told me he'd pay practically anything for a day to himself. I asked him to quantify this statement. "For instance, would you pay $100 for a free day?" I asked. "Sure I would," he responded.

It doesn't take a genius to see where I'm going with this one. Whether it's $100, $50, or $500 isn't the real issue. The real issue is, just how important is it (really) for you to create some time for yourself?

One of the reasons many men can't find any time for themselves is that they try to do everything themselves. And even when they do hire someone else on occasion (or trade services), instead of using the time they just created for themselves, they simply go to the next item on their list.

It's a never-ending cycle. In fact, with this attitude toward doing things, you ensure that you'll never have any time because you'll never get around to finishing everything on your list.

The only solution is to take a hard look at your priorities and make three very important decisions: 1) What things on this list do I want to do myself? 2) Which things on this list can I afford to delegate? And, 3) most importantly, when I delegate something, what do I want to do with the time I save? The third question is the key.

Let's return to the man I met who yearned for a day to himself. If he was willing (and could afford) to have someone else work on his car and/ or fix his toilet, he could then make the decision, in advance, that the time he saved by doing so would be reserved for him and not used to rake the leaves or paint the house. He can plan to do those things the next weekend.

You might ask, Doesn't that mean that he would, in effect, be paying for his time off? Absolutely, but it's often the case that you must pay for something you want. Obviously, if you want to have dinner at a great restaurant, you have to pay for it. Sometimes, if you want to create some free time, you have to pay for it, as well.

Perhaps an excellent trade-off would be to hire someone to change your oil (or fix your toilet, or both), and then not go to a restaurant. If money is an issue, use the time you save to do something that doesn't cost a lot of money.

I'm not suggesting that there aren't certain things you might want to do yourself or that might be too expensive to delegate. I'm only suggesting that you don't have to do everything. And when you discover which things you aren't going to do, you will have just discovered a new way to find time for you.

48

ENGAGE IN LESS
PICKING AND CHOOSING

One of my favorite sayings comes from an author named Seng Ts'an. It says, "Our way is not difficult save the picking and choosing." I interpret this to mean that, if it were not for our vast preferences and our attachment to having to have things be a certain way, life isn't difficult at all.

Easier said than done, of course, but the point is well taken. After all, if not for our insistence that things be the way we want them to be, we would be happy most of the time. If we didn't demand that people react the way we want them to, we would accept them as they are. If we weren't concerned, or at least so consumed with outcomes, we would be free from anxiety and stress.

Philosophically, it's pretty easy to understand this idea—but to put it into practice is a different story. After all, we do have preferences and attachments to outcomes. We want things to turn out in our favor. So what's the trick?

The key seems to be in making an ongoing effort to accept life as it is in any given moment. Rather than thinking things must be different or putting conditions on our own peace of mind, we instead need to drop the need for things to be different and reduce the amount of "picking and choosing" we engage in.

For example, suppose you really want to go on a camping trip this year with your family. You plan it and promote the idea to your wife and kids. You bring home magazines with photos of what you're likely to see. It's really important to you. Unfortunately, you're outnumbered. The rest of the family wants to go to Disneyland. What do you do? Do you sulk, feel resentful, and ripped off? Or do you accept what is and make the decision to have a great time? This is a helpful strategy because, even when the issues are far more important than where you go on vacation, this type of thinking allows you to be peaceful with the way things turn out.

I've found it very helpful to say the words, "It is as it is." These simple words remind me to stop resisting (so much) the way things really are. For example, a friend (or one of my kids, or someone I work with) might not be acting the way I think he or she should be acting. If I remind myself to accept things the way they are—rather than demanding that they be different—I can immediately become less judgmental and reactive. Or if I've just lost money in a business venture, I can let go of it more quickly and move on by accepting the truth as it actually is, rather than spending my time and energy regretting what could have been or beating myself up over any bad decisions I may have made.

Becoming less attached to outcomes doesn't mean that you don't care or that you don't try. Instead, it's more a matter of trying really hard, caring a great deal, putting the odds in your favor—but then letting go of the result and allowing things to unfold as they will (which is what will happen anyway).

I think you'll be shocked at how much easier life will be when you adopt the attitude of less picking and choosing. Who knows? You may turn out to be pretty calm, after all.

49

KEEP IN MIND THAT
NO DECISION IS A DECISION

I was first introduced to this lesson in my senior year in high school. I was procrastinating on making my decision about which colleges to apply for when my father sat me down and said, "Richard, it's ultimately your decision what you want to do. But remember, no decision is a decision." It hit me like a ton of bricks.

What he was suggesting, of course, was that I had every right to continue postponing my decisions and any necessary action required to attend college. However, the act of not acting (that is, not making any concrete decisions) was, in fact, a decision. In every practical sense of the word, it was the same as making the decision not to go to college.

Since that time, many years ago, this simple idea has helped me to make many decisions. It has also greatly reduced my anxiety and stress about certain things because I realize that I'm the one making the decision to make no decision. For example, I had some money in an interest-bearing money market fund. My original intention was to keep it there while I decided what to do with it. It sat there for more than two years, earning an extremely low rate of interest. One day, a friend of mine asked me how I was investing my money. A little embarrassed at my lack of involvement, I confessed that I was waiting to decide. Like my dad, he reminded me that by doing nothing, I had made the decision to receive perhaps the lowest rate of interest that was currently available on the market. The next day, I invested a portion of the money elsewhere.

Remember that if you don't make a decision (or continue to procrastinate in making a decision), that is a decision. It's a choice you're making to not take any action—which usually means that you lose some control over what happens. It's sort of like voting: If you don't exercise your right to vote, you're allowing others to make your political choices for you. On a more personal level that affects your day-to-day living, choosing not to take action or not to make a decision can make you feel powerless over your own life, and, ultimately, can create a great deal of anxiety.

Examples of this are everywhere. Suppose you're getting overweight and are working too hard. It's clear that if you continue on the same path, you're going to jeopardize your health, the way you look, and the way you feel. To simply go on as you are is an example of not making a decision. Therefore, you have just made the decision to adversely affect your life.

Understanding this concept is tremendously empowering because, even if you decide that you're not going to make any changes, at least you're aware of what you're doing. Hopefully, however, where important decisions are involved, you will make the decision to make a decision— to start exercising, making life changes, eating better, investing in a higher-interest earning fund, and so forth.

I hope you'll agree that this is a useful concept that can make your life a whole lot easier and less stressful. Once you know that no decision is a decision, you'll be more equipped to make really good decisions.

50

MEMORIZE THE WORDS, "THERE'S NO SUCH THING AS BAD WEATHER—ONLY DIFFERENT KINDS OF GOOD WEATHER"

At this moment, I'm looking out the window at some beautiful rain. In fact, it's more than raining, it's pouring. The temperature is a chilly 48 degrees, and the local meteorologists are promising snow tonight in the higher elevations of the Bay Area hills, a rare treat for the area in which I live.

It's interesting, however, to notice the reaction most people seem to have to the weather. I'd guess that, today alone, I heard the words, "What horrible weather we're having" (or some variation of those words) at least a dozen times. The folks on the radio—disk jockeys, news reporters, and others—keep talking about how much they hope the weather will get better by tomorrow. As you walk through the streets, you hear the same thing. People are complaining about the weather, wishing it were different, waiting for a better set of facts. Most people seem to assume that there is something wrong with the weather we are having.

I just turned the dial. The weatherman on my favorite station just said the words, "The weather should be improving in the next few days," again reinforcing the idea that the rain is somehow bad and that we should collectively postpone our enjoyment until things get better. It's almost like there's a silent agreement that everyone is supposed to hate the current weather in favor of bright blue skies and perfect picnic weather, which occurs only every once in a while. But the rest of the days, we should wait and complain. No one is supposed to enjoy the weather we are having, appreciate the diversity, or marvel at what Mother Nature has in store for today. Nope, it's simply not good enough.

I'm kidding, of course, but what makes it all so funny to me is that this is one of the first rains of the season, and we're really in desperate need of rain. The ground is dry, and the area is known for some horrible fires this time of the year. Truthfully, nothing is more important right now, weather-wise, than a healthy dose of rain.

When you think about it, it's easy to see that there isn't really any kind of bad weather, only different kinds of good weather. It's just that the conditions are good for very different reasons. We need it all—sun, rain, snow, even wind to spread the seeds of flowers and trees. Have you ever been to a desert? Can you imagine what the world would be like with no rain? There's a mountain on Kauai in the Hawaiian Islands that is, allegedly, one of the wettest places on earth. It almost never stops raining. It's absolutely beautiful in the surrounding areas, but can you imagine what it would be like if that was all there was, weather-wise? Try telling a ski enthusiast that snow is bad or a windsurfer that we can do without wind. It's all necessary, and it's all perfect in its own way.

It would be difficult for me to guess what the most common complaint of the average person is; there are so many to choose from. I'd have to say, though, that way up there on the list is something we have absolutely no control over—the weather.

I bring the issue of weather to your attention, not because it's that big a deal, but because our resistance to it is symbolic of our resistance to life in general. So often, instead of being open and accepting of whatever we are experiencing, we resist it, push it away, and demand that it be different. But like fighting the weather, it's a losing battle.

Why not instead simply accept and enjoy the weather you are having, whatever it happens to be? After all, the weather is what it is anyway, and it certainly doesn't care what you or I think about it. If it's hot and humid, that's what it's going to be until it changes. If it's cold and windy, it's going to go on being cold and windy until conditions reverse.

As you extend your acceptance of the weather into other areas of your life, you'll observe a noticeable change in the way you feel. Acceptance reduces pressure and anxiety. As you embrace what's going on in life instead of demanding that it be somehow different, you'll spend far less time being frustrated because you'll be so much more open, accepting, and interested in what's really going on.

51

TRY THE "PAUSE AND
COME BACK TO IT" TECHNIQUE

To one degree or another, everyone gets angry, frustrated, anxious, agitated, bothered, irritated, stressed, and every other conceivable negative emotion. It's amazing, however, how quickly many of these emotions fade away if we simply give them some time.

In and of themselves, the impulses or automatic reactions we feel aren't problematic. They usually only become problematic if we act on them.

A few days ago, I was stood up for a meeting. As much as I try to not sweat it, I found myself getting more and more irritated by the minute! I had rearranged my schedule to accommodate this person and was, quite frankly, doing him a favor. In addition, I had reconfirmed the meeting that morning.

Ten or fifteen years ago, I would have left the restaurant in an angry huff, probably calculating how much his mistake had cost me. There's no question that I would have been having a thought attack, one of those angry conversations within my own head.

This time, however, something very simple came to my rescue. I call it the "pause and come back to it" technique. Simply put, you make the choice to let something go now, and if necessary, to come back to whatever is bugging you—later. The beauty of this process is that by the time later comes around, you're usually completely over it (whatever it was), and you couldn't care less.

By making the decision to come back to it later, you are, in effect, postponing any (over)reaction you might be having. You're not saying, "I won't get angry" (frustrated, jealous, anxious, or whatever), but instead, that you'll do so at a later time. I've found that, more often than not, the simple acknowledgment that it might be a good idea to wait takes the sting out of whatever is going on in that moment.

I've incorporated this "go ahead and get angry later" technique into my life with amazing results. The concept is simple. You give yourself permission to get as angry or as frustrated as you'd like—with one condition: You clear your mind, forget about it, and get on with your day or evening. That's it. If, two hours later, you're still angry—then go ahead and be angry. Feel as badly as you want.

I say this because the percentage of time you'll actually take yourself up on this offer is minuscule. I've used this technique many times and can't think of a single instance in which I've felt more than mildly irritated two hours later. The truth is that if your anger or frustration is justified or super important, it will still be there hours later—so what do you have to lose? The worst that can happen is that you will have had a chance to cool off and gain some much-needed perspective. That way, you'll end up dealing with the situation from a much better frame of mind.

One word of warning: This won't work if you spend the two hours stewing over whatever it is you're upset about. In order for this to work, you have to clear your mind and forget about it.

This strategy works great with virtually anything. You might be irritated with your spouse, child, or girlfriend. Or, something happens at work—or important plans are thwarted—or someone messes up, or whatever. The next time life dishes out an unexpected hassle, don't sweat it! Try the "pause and come back to it" technique. It will work if you'll give it a try.

52

REMEMBER THAT SOMETIMES LESS EFFORT IS BETTER

I love the simple Zen statement, "Spring comes and the grass grows all by itself." What a powerful reminder that, sometimes, it's best to allow things to unfold in their own way, without too much effort on our part.

During a recent conversation, a friend of mine shared with me that he was furious with his daughter. After sharing the details with me, he told me of his intention to hash it out with her later that evening. I asked him if he would consider waiting a few days before discussing things with her. After some initial objections, he agreed.

By putting some time and space between his initial reaction and his confrontation, the edge was removed, as was the bulk of his anger. He softened. His compassion and wisdom returned. By doing essentially nothing, he was able to have a healing heart-to-heart conversation with his daughter. Rather than lecturing her and driving a wedge even deeper between them, he was able to listen intently to what she had to say. He remembered what it was like to be a teenager himself. By the end of the conversation, they were close again.

Often, when someone is mad at me, I attempt to implement this strategy. Rather than trying to explain myself, which often compounds or exacerbates a problem, I allow the person to vent their frustration. Usually, that's all it takes. In fact, the less effort, the better.

Friendships as well as intimate relationships are like that, too. When you force them, or try too hard, you can end up pushing someone away. Ironically, your well-intended actions can backfire. By allowing relationships to unfold, in their own time and in their own way, a magical connection has a chance to develop.

Like most men, there are times when I simply don't know what to do. I'm confused and don't have a good answer. What I've learned is that, in these instances, less effort is usually better. Rather than struggle for an answer, make one up, or pretend I have one, I instead choose to back off and allow things to unfold. I used to be amazed at how often this seemingly passive approach would somehow turn out to be the best way to proceed. Lately, however, I've discovered that this approach to life is not as passive as it seems at first glance. Instead, allowing things to unfold, instead of forcing the issue or struggling to make something happen, is the path of wisdom and, often, the path of least resistance.

53

EASE UP BEHIND THE WHEEL

In *Don't Sweat the Small Stuff*, I included a chapter called "Become a Less Aggressive Driver." Since that time, it has become even more apparent to me that easing up behind the wheel is one of the most important and immediate ways to reduce stress and live a more peaceful life.

To begin with, many of us spend a great deal of time in our cars—one, two, even three hours a day isn't at all unusual. But even if you don't spend a lot of time behind the wheel, whenever you're a driver, or a passenger, it's important to keep your cool.

My family and I love to spend time on the California coast. Just yesterday, I was driving home on the long, winding (and very dangerous) road back to the Bay Area. A man in a pickup truck came up behind me at a stop sign. Apparently, I wasn't driving as fast as he would have liked me to, so he honked at me and gave me an angry look and a wave of his finger. Without looking in either direction, he sped around me, obviously furious with my lack of hurry. I could see him racing recklessly down the hill, totally oblivious to the fact that he was never more than a few feet away from wiping out entire families.

About ten minutes later, driving at exactly the same speed I had all morning, I came up behind him at the next stop. In fact, there were fewer cars in my lane, so I actually passed him on the left. One of my kids pointed out that he pretended not to see us, and she believed he felt embarrassed about the fact that his reckless driving hadn't gotten him any farther down the road.

As hard as it is to believe sometimes, the difference between how long it takes when you speed impatiently from place to place versus how long the same trip takes when you drive the legal speed limit is minimal. Approached in a more peaceful manner, however, the identical trip turns out to be an entirely different experience.

When you ease up behind the wheel, several things happen. First, because you're driving more slowly and carefully, you can relax a little. You don't have to worry about passing cars around blind corners or about police officers who might spot you. As a result, you experience less stress.

By taking just a few extra seconds, you'll be contributing to a safer highway. Who knows how many lives you'll save or how many accidents you'll avoid? Instead of gripping the wheel, feeling tense, and speeding around corners, slow down a little and listen to some nice music or a good audio book. Driving can actually be a relaxing experience.

Finally—and most ironically—in the long run, you'll spend less time involved in car-related issues if you ease up behind the wheel. The reason is that you'll be in fewer accidents and will get far fewer traffic tickets over your lifetime. It would take a lot of dangerous speeding to make up for just one day in traffic school. All things considered, it's simply not worth it.

54

QUIET DOWN

This is a book that was written to help you reduce stress and live a happier life. Yet even if your only goal was to become super-successful or rich and famous, I'd still suggest learning to quiet down. Likewise, if your primary concern was to feel less overwhelmed or to prioritize better, I'd make the same suggestion. If you were trying to figure out how to improve the quality of your relationships, again, I'd try to convince you to learn to quiet down. It's that important, and it's that useful.

Our lives are filled to capacity. We have many responsibilities, conflicting agendas, and things to keep track of. We have goals, dreams, plans, and obligations. At any given moment, we might have hundreds of things going on.

When we compound our multitude of tasks and responsibilities with an equally frenetic and busy mind, the result is confusion, chaos, and stress. It's sort of like trying to do an important task that requires total concentration, while at the same time, having ten or twelve people shouting at you, firing requests at you, and yelling out, "Hurry, hurry, look at your watch!"—all at the same time.

Any task, when attempted with a quiet mind, is substantially easier.

Without the distraction of busyness, chatter, and confusion, you're usually able to accomplish a lot. You see what needs to be done much more clearly.

When your mind is quiet, it's as though everything settles down. Life appears to come at you much more slowly, when in reality, of course, it doesn't. You seem to have more time, and you're able to keep your bearings. Because you're so much less reactive, you're less inclined to panic or make mistakes. You're easier to work with, and you're easier on yourself.

Life appears to be more orderly when you have a quiet mind. The chaos doesn't get to you as much. You're able to see the bigger picture, and you're able to prioritize much more effectively. Rather than spending your time putting out fires and attending to emergencies, you're able to differentiate between that which only seems like an emergency and that which really is an emergency. It's hard to believe until you've experienced it, but when you quiet down, you'll actually get far more accomplished with a quieter mind than you will with a frantic one. This is particularly true of important things. Rather than forcing events to happen, you'll find yourself allowing things to happen. Ideas will come to you, as if from out of the blue.

Quieting down is a mind-set, not a set of circumstances. There are plenty of people with relatively few actual emergencies to deal with, who are freaked out and stressed almost all of the time. There are others who deal with extraordinarily stressful things, but who are able to take most of it in stride.

The key to quieting down lies in your intent. If you perceive that quieting down would be advantageous, you'll be able to move in that direction.

If you attach value to a quieter mind instead of assuming that it would create problems (such as losing your edge or sense of competitiveness, the most common fears), it will be easier to calm down.

Becoming more inwardly quiet can come about in several ways. You can learn a formal skill such as meditation or yoga, which can be quite helpful. As you practice, the benefits will spread into your daily life. Or, if you prefer, you can attempt to quiet down by simply beginning to notice when you are more speeded up or when there's too much noise in your head.

Pay attention to how you are feeling. If you're feeling stressed and your mind is going in ten directions at once, it's a good indication that you're moving too quickly. At times like these, take a breath, step back, and consciously begin to quiet down. As you get used to the new mental pace, you'll find yourself enjoying it more and more.

I once was asked if a person could ever become "too quiet" for his own good. I responded by saying that I don't think many men would have to worry about that. In my opinion, most of us could benefit from becoming a little quieter. I, myself, have a long way to go. How about you?

55

HAVE A SPARE SET

It was two hours before my plane took off. I was on my way out of my house to promote a book, and I was taking the last flight of the day. My home is about an hour away from the San Francisco Airport. There was no backup flight, and no way to reschedule. I was getting ready to leave when I realized what had happened . . . I had lost my essential stuff—my wallet and keys! Time to panic? No way.

A long time ago I realized how easy it would be for something like this to happen. Think about how many times you scramble to locate your important things. If you've never actually lost your things, chances are, you probably will at some point. The only question is, when? Will it be on your way to the airport or on your way out the door to an important meeting? Will you be taking a client out to lunch? Or will it happen thirty minutes before a hot date? And even if you never actually lose your things, they could conceivably be stolen.

Imagine what a terrible inconvenience and hassle it will be—unless you're prepared. The funny thing is, being prepared takes close to no effort.

I have an extra set of keys tucked away in a drawer. It's not a partial set, but a copy of every single key I own. Alongside the keys is a spare wallet with a credit card and a little cash, ready to go—just in case. Since

I know I'll need a photo ID whenever I'm flying, I keep my passport in the same place.

When I discovered that I had misplaced my things, rather than panic, I simply walked to where I keep everything, grabbed my extra set, and walked out the door. No reason to worry or make a big deal out of it. I knew it was likely my things would show up—and they did, a few days later—but even if they didn't, I knew it would be fine.

I have to admit that when I created my "spare set," I thought I was being a little neurotic. How paranoid, I thought to myself. But then I realized that it's not that much different from having an emergency earthquake supply, which we have, as well—food, flashlights, batteries, a radio, water, blankets, stuff like that—just in case.

So many people—men and women—have told me how worried they get when they can't find their wallet, purse, or keys. Even though it's not big stuff, it still creates enormous anxiety because it usually happens at the worst possible moment. It's very different, however, when you know that you have a spare set. In a very practical way, it keeps you from sweating it.

As long as you're being prepared, you may want to consider some sort of a credit card registry as well. Or, at very least, having access to all your credit card numbers and the phone numbers to call in case they ever need to be canceled. A good idea might be to photocopy all the contents of your wallet so you can know immediately what was in there if you ever lose it. One final thing to consider is a home video and photos of all your valuable things in the event of fire or theft. About a year after we moved from our previous home, the Oakland Hills fire destroyed the house we used to own. It was one of the worst fires in American history, burning hundreds of homes to the ground. Although we didn't need it anymore, the new owners were thrilled when we contacted them to let them know we had a video of the home that they were welcome to use if they needed it for insurance purposes. They used it.

Obviously, you want to keep all these things in a really safe place, and, in the case of the video, somewhere other than the house you're filming. In any event, I encourage you to do this sooner rather than later. Hopefully, you'll never actually need your "spare set," yet this is one of those strategies where sweating the details a little bit can help you stop sweating the small stuff—and from worrying for years to come.

56

ANTICIPATE THE BEST

Three times this week, in three different cities, I heard a man say the words, "It's important to anticipate the worst." Each time, it was said in a conclusive manner, as if this was somehow a wise statement.

Benjamin Franklin once said, "I imagined some horrible things in my life—a few of which actually occurred." Most of us do the same thing. We worry, fret, get bothered, all worked up, and bent out of shape. The trouble is, a vast majority of the time, things work out anyway. So what's the point of spending so much time and energy imagining all these horrible things?

Consider, for a moment, the illogic of always assuming the worst. If what Franklin said is true, then most things will turn out fine. However, we tend to assume that they will not turn out fine. In fact, despite strong evidence to the contrary, we're going to assume that everything is going to go to hell in a handbasket. So, instead of easing through life—knowing that if we do our best and put the odds in our favor, all will be well most of the time—we're instead going to be stressed out and frantic for no legitimate reason. We're going to plan for the worst, spend our time and energy figuring out what to do if the walls come crumbling down, have intense conversations in our minds about all that could go wrong, and remain tense, agitated, and on guard. We're going to anticipate the worst.

Obviously, I'm not suggesting that that you don't think through the issues in your life, or plan ahead. Like you, I have contingency plans, I'm careful, and I carry life insurance. It's not about failing to plan, but instead it's about choosing to not spend your life immobilized and frightened about things that aren't likely to happen or those over which you have no control. One thing is certain: If you can eliminate (or greatly reduce) being worried about these two types of concerns, you're on to something important. You'll be far less stressed on a day-to-day basis, and you'll be a much happier person.

I hope you'll think about this strategy and give it a fair shot. You can certainly start with small issues, but I encourage you to start today. Instead of assuming that your conversation is going to be adversarial, assume it will result in a peaceful resolution. Instead of assuming someone is out to get you or take advantage of you, work on the assumption that most people are honest and that things will work out fine. You'll quickly discover that, most of the time, your new assumptions are going to be correct. I think you'll find that assuming the best is the best way to live.

57

BE SURE YOU'RE MAD AT WHAT
YOU THINK YOU ARE

A woman shared with me the fact that while she and her husband were in therapy, they discovered something that probably saved their marriage. Since the early days of their marriage, this woman's husband had taken on a "I won't be controlled by a woman" attitude. He had become so militant in his position that he refused to participate in family life. When she would ask him to share his time or complain that he wasn't doing enough, he would become cold and distant. In an angry tone, he would say things like, "I'm going to play golf" or "I'm working late." His tone and implication was, "Don't question me or my motives."

It turned out that this woman's husband had grown up with an extremely controlling mother who monitored his every move. Consciously or unconsciously, he had vowed to himself that it would never happen again: he would never, ever, allow a woman—any woman—to tell him what to do or how to act. The result was that he had become extremely defensive and reactive to even the slightest degree of expectation or even the most reasonable of requests pertaining to his marriage or his family. It was getting worse, not better.

Interestingly enough, this woman's husband was a kind person and a talented professional. The issue wasn't that his wife felt she or the kids weren't loved, but rather that his unshakable, stubborn resistance to obligation was becoming a real drag on the family. He was so stuck on that single issue that it was interfering with any fun that he or his family might otherwise be able to enjoy.

What they jointly discovered in therapy was that the woman's requests were quite minimal and reasonable. It became obvious to him that unlike his mother many years earlier, his wife had no secret desire or need to control him at all. Instead, it turned out that what he was reacting to had little or nothing to do with her. Instead, he had taken his feelings of being smothered and controlled as a child into his adult life. The way he put it was, "I was mad at my mother."

Believe me when I say that I'm totally against psychobabble, and don't understand most of it myself. I think we can overanalyze our relationships to death, and, in doing so, hurt the very things we are trying to mend. However, over the years, I've met and known some really great therapists and have come to accept the fact that there are times when a neutral third party, or some sort of counselor, can do wonders for a committed relationship.

A good therapist is able to encourage us to see things about ourselves that we might not otherwise be able to see. He or she can help us create a nondefensive atmosphere where we can explore our feelings and find out what's really going on. Ideally, a therapist will help us tap into our own inner wisdom so we can live a life of love and insight. He or she can help us break any destructive habits that have crept into our relationship and can even help us rekindle our love for our partner. These things can happen, even if you choose to talk to someone all by yourself. With a little help, it's sometimes easier to become more reflective and philosophical.

I've caught myself many times feeling angry toward someone, only to discover later—after being more reflective about it—that I was actually mad at someone else, or even mad at myself. Years ago, for example, there was a period of time when I was mad at Kris because she was able to schedule time to spend with her friends and to do fun things, and I wasn't. What I discovered, however, was that I wasn't mad at Kris at all. Instead, I was mad at myself for not prioritizing time for myself.

Once the truth is out in the open, or you become aware of it, it's much easier to let go of whatever or whomever you're really angry with. When it's unclear what's really going on, you can spend a lot of time being tense. But when you discover the truth by becoming more reflective, it's easier to stop sweating the small stuff and let go of being so mad and stressed.

58

EXPERIENCE THE POWER OF
BEING PRESENT

One of the most amazing things I've ever observed was the instant transformation that occurred to a man who was very depressed. Someone brought a baby into the room and, for a few minutes, the man forgot he was depressed. He lit up with enthusiasm as he held and played with the adorable little person. As a passive observer, you could see the seriousness and worry fade away, replaced with a genuine and heartwarming smile.

About ten minutes later, the baby started crying and his mother decided she'd better go feed the hungry guy. So, she carefully and gently took the baby from the man and walked away.

In an instant, you could see the concern returning to the man's face. Whereas a minute before he was glowing in the present moment, totally absorbed in the beauty and wonder of what he was doing, his mind now seemed once again to return to his habit of thinking about his life—instead of living in the moments of his life.

Being present is one of the most talked-about mental dynamics in spiritual life, and, I believe, may be the single most important concept of living if your goal is to be happy and effective. In the absence of being present, you live in a world of fear, anticipation, regret, anxiety, and stress. Your mind takes you back into the past, reminding you of painful times and your world of troubles, as well as off into the future, encouraging you to worry and fret.

When you are present, your mind is clear. You see things as they really are, in that moment. Your mind isn't distracted by its thoughts of what might happen or the motives of other people. It's not cluttered with suspicions, fears, or worries. Nor is it contaminated with painful memories from the past—regrets or reminders of negative experiences.

Instead, when you are present, you simply attend to what you are doing or who you are within a clear mental environment. Your mind is fully absorbed and attentive to the present moment. If you are with another person, you are listening deeply and respectfully rather than allowing your mind to wander elsewhere.

Unfortunately, becoming more present isn't something that happens by reading a few paragraphs about it. Despite being a simple concept, it definitely takes some practice. It's one of those things that needs to be experienced to be fully appreciated.

We're all like the man who was depressed, then wasn't, then was again. When our mind is wandering here and there, contemplating problems, becoming absorbed and caught up in various dramas, we experience the feelings associated with those thoughts—confusion, fear, anger, worry, anxiety, and so forth. It's like we get lost in the contents of our own thinking, and, for the most part, we're not even aware it's happening. It just happens, automatically.

We have the power, however, to recognize our own thinking when it's taking us places we don't want or need to go. When we do, we're able to bring our attention back to the moment—to whatever we are doing or whomever we are with. You'll notice that when you can do this, you'll experience whatever you're dealing with far less stressfully. It's like waking up from a bad dream and saying, "Wow, I was really off somewhere." The only difference is, your dream is happening while you are awake.

Being present reduces the stress you feel, even when you're dealing with a serious problem. Years ago, while in college, my wife, Kris, experienced the hardship of having her dorm room destroyed in a fire. She certainly had to deal with the fact that virtually all her belongings were destroyed, yet her ability to stay present with the experience prevented her from falling into despair.

You can imagine that in a situation like this, many people allow their minds to spin out of control toward the future and think of all the negative implications and horrible scenarios. Their minds then flip to the past as they remember the photographs and all the special items that can't be replaced. Their minds spin back and forth from the pain of the lost items to the anticipated pain likely to occur in the future.

In the meantime, however, here you are in the moment. In Kris's case, she was extremely fortunate that neither she nor anyone else was hurt.

The fire is out. Once it's over, the pain is being created by all the thoughts associated with the fire. The power of this understanding is awesome. It allows you to deal with life, including painful events, without become totally overwhelmed by them.

Please understand that I'm not minimizing this, or any other serious incident. A fire is a potentially deadly tragedy. Being present is not in any way about pretending that you don't care about these things—instead, it's about seeing how we all contribute to, and exacerbate, the painful (and not so painful) experiences in our lives by failing to recognize when our mind is taking us to horrible or painful places.

We do the same thing with so many aspects of our lives. We might, for example, be doing okay financially, but worry ourselves sick about retirement. Again, being more present is not a prescription for failing to plan for your future, but rather a way of moving through your life effectively without allowing your mind to ruin your experience or overmagnify your problems.

You can imagine how effective this can be when you're dealing with the ordinary events of day-to-day living. Events, people, and situations that usually drive you nuts will be experienced with far more ease. By practicing being more present-moment oriented, you'll create a peace of mind that you'll carry with you throughout your life. As events unfold, you'll deal with them effectively and wisely, while at the same time keeping your stress levels under control.

59

IDENTIFY YOUR STRESS SIGNALS

I was having some back pain and discussed with a physician what might be wrong. What I found out was enlightening. He told me that, while my physical symptoms were very real and must be attended to, when I was feeling too stressed, the pain might flare up even worse.

I started paying attention to this mind-body connection and have discovered that, for me, it does indeed exist. In other words, when my thoughts drift too far toward anger, seriousness, fear, or negativity, I actually feel it in my back. My back pain is a signal letting me know that I'm getting too stressed. It reminds me to take my thoughts a little less seriously, to lighten up and slow down.

Recognizing this connection has proven to be a reliable way for me to monitor my own level of stress and then make adjustments that can help. When my back feels really stiff, it might be that it's time for me to take a few deep breaths or a brisk walk. In my case, it usually means that I've gotten too caught up in my thinking and it's time to back off a little.

Many men have told me of similar patterns in other areas of their bodies. Sometimes it's a stiffness in their neck that only shows up when they're under stress. Other times it's a feeling in the pit of their stomach or a clenching of the jaw or the fists.

Does this mean it's all in your head? No, of course not. You should always check with your physician first and often, to be sure any physical symptoms are taken care of. And while you're at it, check with him or her to see whether they feel there might be any connection between your physical pain and stress.

What I'm suggesting is nonmedical and subtle. It's about learning to identify and pay attention to the feelings you have—physical and emotional—and to see if there is any connection between the feelings you are having and the stress you are feeling.

I was talking to a cardiologist after an evening lecture. He told me that he had learned to identify his stress signals by recognizing a feeling of agitation that would start to dominate his mind-set. Prior to making this connection, he would feel the agitation, then roll up his sleeves and work even harder and faster. His stress would escalate, and he felt like he was going to go crazy. He said he felt like a hamster on a wheel. When he felt stressed, he would run even faster—which made him feel more stress, which would encourage him to run faster still. And so on.

Everything began to change for him when he realized that the feeling of agitation was actually a good thing. It was like a friend saying to him, "Okay, here we go again. You're getting too uptight. It's time to back off a bit and regain your perspective." He said that as long as he pays attention to these agitated feelings, he's usually able to listen to what they are trying to tell him. He also said that there's no question that his overall level of stress has diminished significantly.

If you start paying attention to your feelings, you might be surprised at what they are trying to tell you. If you're feeling stressed, it means you're having stressful thoughts. If you're feeling resentful or overwhelmed, it suggests you're having those kinds of thoughts, and so forth. By making the connection between the feelings you experience and the stress you're feeling, you can make some mental adjustments that can ease the problem.

60

BECOME MORE ACCEPTING
OF CHANGE

Although change is one of the only certainties in life, it remains, for most of us, one of the most difficult aspects to deal with. Whether we like it or not, we're always dealing with some aspect of change. Our bodies are changing; our kids are growing up; our relationships change, as do the business environment and markets. The economy changes, as does the weather. Neighborhoods change, as do our circumstances. Sometimes, change happens very slowly—whereas other times, it happens in an instant.

Because change is so absolutely certain, it pays huge dividends to learn to become more accepting of its many forms. Easier said than done, of course, but still worth any effort you put into it. In fact, if you can learn to be more accepting of change in all aspects of your life, you will find yourself sweating the small stuff (and the big stuff) far less often.

Consider your alternative. If, instead of becoming more accepting of change, you fight and resist with all your might, you'll find yourself suffering. Suppose, for example, you refuse to acknowledge that your kids are growing up. Good luck on that one. The truth is, they are growing up, so now what? You can deny it—but it doesn't change the reality of life.

I turned forty this year. No amount of my wishing it were otherwise could have changed my birthday. I had two options: embrace change or suffer and feel badly about it. It's the same dynamic whether you're turning thirty, fifty, seventy, or ninety. We are always faced with the same choice—embrace or suffer.

Most changes are far more subtle, but equally important to embrace. For example, moods change in people (including in ourselves). If you can only be happy when someone is acting a certain way, you'll be disappointed a great deal of the time. On the other hand, if you can be okay with the changing moods that people have (even your own), you'll live with more peace of mind. Your openness to change enables you to go with the flow of life.

Embracing change is an important concept of certain spiritual traditions. You could spend an entire lifetime learning about and practicing this wisdom. I won't, for a moment, pretend to have the ultimate answers. However, from my perspective, the essential keys are twofold.

First, it's important to see the necessity of change. Without it, we could not exist. If your kids didn't grow up, they couldn't have kids of their own. If we didn't get both rain and sunshine, the plants wouldn't grow, and so forth. When we hang on to things beyond a certain point—youth, beauty, power, a role, success, or whatever—we suffer. On the other hand, when you see the necessity of change, you feel at peace. A champion athlete is a joy to see. However, it's necessary, at some point, for that athlete to step aside so that another can take his or her place. It's the way of things.

Reflecting on the necessity of change helps us see the perfection of life *as it is* instead of as it was or as it should be. Going back to our children for a moment, they were beautiful as infants, as toddlers, and as youngsters. They will be equally beautiful as teens and as adults. The change doesn't diminish the beauty; it merely changes its form.

The second key relates to the first. It has to do with our expectations surrounding change. It's interesting to notice the fear and dread that often accompanies our thoughts about change. We think, "Oh no, I'm getting older," or "Retirement is coming—what will I do then?" Not always, but often, we assume that change is going to be difficult, bad, or painful, which creates a self-fulfilling prophecy. If we can minimize the fear and negativity surrounding change, and instead approach it with a sense of openness and wonder, we reduce or even eliminate the fear. In other words, if we can think to ourselves, "Here's change taking place," instead of "Oh no, change!" that subtle shift can make a world of difference. It's the difference between being interested in and accepting of the change and being anxious or frustrated by it.

Remember, change is going to be there whether you like it or not. What we're left with is the degree to which we embrace change or push it away. This is one of those philosophical issues that is important to reflect upon. To me, it seems the more peaceful we become about change in general, the happier we will be.

61

REFLECT ON THE POWER
OF PREVENTION

I've always found it much easier to prevent certain things from happening than to fix or repair them after the fact. This applies to everything from health-related issues, to business decisions, and even personal relationships. By reminding yourself of the power of prevention and implementing its wisdom into your life, you can save yourself a great deal of grief, and, in the process, reduce some of the stress you experience.

It's easier for me, for example, to keep my weight down rather than to lose weight. Knowing this makes it easier for me to say no to certain foods or to avoid excessive quantities. I simply remind myself that it's not worth the trade-off. The same applies to exercise. As hard as it can be to find the time, it's still much easier to prioritize some regular exercise—and stay in shape—than it is to try to get back into shape after weeks or months of nonactivity. Reminding myself of this simple truth sparks my energy level and resolve to exercise.

The same seems true in many business-related ventures. By attending to details up front, right from the start (even if they are a hassle), you can prevent problems down the road. A background or reference check, for example, could in certain instances uncover information that would convince you not to hire someone. In this scenario, you might be preventing problems down the line. In addition, by practicing ongoing ethical business practices today, you create the necessary goodwill that can help you for years to come. I believe it's much easier to keep your clients and customers happy than it is to make them happy once they are angry or disappointed. This is simple wisdom, but the payoff is tremendous.

I've found that the idea of prevention also applies to my personal relationships. In other words, by taking the time to make love and friendship a true priority today, I can keep my most important relationships and my friendships intact. In other words, spending time with my kids right now, today—even if I'm really busy—not only makes all of us happy, but it's also ensures that we'll have a relationship tomorrow. Sadly, I've met quite a number of men who have told me, "By the time I realized how important my wife (or kids) were to me, it was too late." Along the same lines, I'd much rather maintain a great relationship with Kris in simple ways on a day-to-day basis than to try to make it up to her by taking her out for a fancy dinner on our anniversary.

These are just a few of the ways that prevention can make our lives better and easier. I'm sure that, if you think about your own life, you'll discover, as I have, the power of prevention.

62

REDEFINE THE WORD

"EMERGENCY"

I can't tell you how many times I've heard the word "emergency" tossed around rather loosely by men over the past several years. There's no doubt in my mind that sometimes there really is an emergency to deal with. There's equally no doubt in my mind, however, that there are many instances in which the word "emergency" is used to describe what, in reality, might be more accurately described as a hassle or an inconvenience. Truthfully, many of us tend to think of things as emergencies, or at least treat them as such, when it's probably not necessary to do so.

I was talking to a group of men when Bob approached the group to announce that there was a crisis he had to go deal with at work—a real emergency. He looked frantic and very concerned. The attention of the group shifted to him and his concerns. He pulled out his cell phone and called his wife to let her know that he would be working very late. The whole scene was very dramatic.

I don't want to minimize his (or anyone else's) concerns, and I never did find out all the facts. However, I was assured by one of his colleagues that the emergency was, in fact, not serious in nature and was something that he had to deal with frequently. Apparently, Bob had a tendency to treat daily problems as slightly more urgent than they really were. Who among us hasn't done that?

The problem with overusing the word "emergency" is that, by doing so, we reinforce the notion that life is incredibly stressful and that we must be on guard all the time. This belief keeps us tense and reactive, even when it's totally unnecessary. Sometimes, thinking about things as emergencies can give us a feeling of self-importance, as if the things we deal with are urgent and require all our attention. This seems to be especially true if we share the emergency with others.

On the other hand, if we can get in the habit of thinking about and responding to life in a slightly less dramatic way, it can help us keep our perspective, see the bigger picture, and respond with more wisdom and equanimity. We may lose some of the attention we receive for always having to deal with urgent matters, but, on the other hand, we might be seen as someone who is calm and collected.

The question is, What is an emergency? It's certainly easy to think of someone else's emergency as less urgent than our own. I'm sure there are many things I overreact to and stress about that you might think of as relatively benign, and vice versa. If we're honest about it, most of us would probably agree that something that is truly dangerous or life-threatening is an emergency, but most other things are not.

The trick is to have the humility to keep reminding ourselves that there are times that we tend to overreact. Ask yourself questions like: "Is this really an emergency—or can it wait?" "Do I absolutely have to get back to the office tonight (and miss my son's party), or can it wait until the morning?" "Is this worth being bothered by or losing sleep over—or is there a simpler solution?" and "Is it possible that I'm making a bigger deal out of this than it really is?"

I still treat certain things as if they were emergencies when it's clear (with the benefit of hindsight) that they never were. But, since asking myself these types of questions, I'm happy to say that it happens less often than it used to. And even when I do make a bigger deal out of something than necessary, I'm often able to downgrade my so-called emergency to a more manageable level.

Most of us have times when we treat small stuff like it's really big stuff. From my perspective, the more often we catch ourselves doing so, the better off we will be. By treating actual emergencies as emergencies and everything else as nonemergencies, we will be less inclined to sweat the small stuff—and we will live happier and more effective lives.

63

DEVELOP SOME NONNEGOTIABLES

I was talking to a man about my intent to write a strategy about nonnegotiables. His response was interesting. He said, "That seems a bit weird. To me, 'nonnegotiable' means stubborn, rigid, and inflexible. That sort of seems like the opposite of what you usually talk about."

"That's true," I said, "but it seems to me that there are certain things that are really good ideas. The problem is, we only seem to get to them or prioritize them when 'everything else is done and taken care of' (which, of course, it rarely is), so we end up not doing those things—at least not as much as we'd like to." Over the years, I've learned that, no matter how hard I try, there is almost never any time left over to do the things I really want to do. By the time I've attended to all of my obligations and responsibilities, there's not much time left.

As I spoke to other men, I discovered most of them have similar stories. So, what I've done is to turn some of those things that I really want to do into nonnegotiables in my mind. In other words, I've decided that it's not negotiable whether I do these things, which makes them, by definition, top priorities.

Most of us have at least a few things that we wish we would prioritize, but don't. A few of my own nonnegotiables include time with my family, exercise, yoga, and meditation. Because I'm certain that, except under unusual circumstances, I'm going to spend at least some time each week doing these things, I tend to plan other things (including meetings, phone calls, and work) around them—not the other way around. Rather than fitting them in, they are automatically prioritized. And it's absolutely amazing to me that when something is a priority, I can find time to do it—and everything else somehow gets done, as well.

Obviously, there are days when it's more difficult than others to stick with my nonnegotiables. Even then, however, I usually find a way to spend at least some time on those activities, which seems to make everything else I do that much more effective and fun.

Not too long ago, I spent most of the day on an airplane that had been delayed. When I finally arrived at my hotel, it was pretty late at night. I remember thinking to myself, "I'll bet if I were to spend even fifteen minutes working out, I'd sleep better and feel better in the morning." And although it would have been much easier to simply turn on the television and order room service, I made myself do it—and boy, was I glad I did. Right away, I felt much better and more relaxed. The point is, if I thought of exercise as something to do when it was convenient, rather than as a nonnegotiable, there would always be good reasons to not do it.

I have a friend who takes a nature hike virtually every day. It doesn't seem to matter what's going on or how much she has to do that day. She always sets aside the time for her walk, and I've always admired her for it. It sure hasn't got in her way, either. She's happy, super-successful, and excels in her career.

I once spoke to a man who had been working in a chaotic environment for more than twenty years. I asked him how he had kept his sanity and good attitude all this time. He said, "For me, it's pretty simple. I always take a lunch break, and spend at least a half-hour all by myself, absolutely alone and away from others. As long as I do this for myself, the rest of my day goes great." His alone time at lunch was nonnegotiable.

I know other people who absolutely, positively won't work on the weekends. It's nonnegotiable. That's their family time, and unless something is truly an emergency, they are committed to keeping that time sacred. It's nice to see too, in some cases, how much their kids and wives appreciate their commitment, as well. Men who do this are just as busy and value their work just as much as you or I do; yet they know where to draw the line. And I, for one, really respect them for taking that stance.

Whatever is most important and nourishing to you can fall into your own nonnegotiable category. By honoring yourself (or your family) in this way, you can create a more peaceful and satisfying life.

64

AVOID OVERIDENTIFYING
WITH YOUR ROLE

I'd have to say that, in my opinion, overidentifying with one's role(s) in life is one of the biggest challenges we face as men. It's also one of the ways we create enormous pain for ourselves—and it's extremely common.

I was at a corporate event when I was introduced to Dan. He said to me, "Nice to meet you. I'm Dan, marketing director." As we walked around the room, Dan constantly referred to himself as "marketing director." It was clear that he saw himself not as Dan, but as Dan the marketing director.

I wasn't able to write this strategy without sounding like I was making fun of this tendency. I'm not. I'm not poking fun at Dan or anyone else who is proud of what they do for a living. Instead, what I'd like to do is to try to distinguish between who we are and what we do. There is an important difference. And being aware of the difference can be an enormous contributor toward peace of mind and contentment.

I once heard Wayne Dyer say, "When you are what you do—then when you don't, you aren't." The message hit loud and clear. We are so much more than what we happen to do for a living. We are spiritual beings—we have roles and responsibilities here on earth, but we are not those roles.

I was talking to a dear friend who was giving up her role as a business person. She had been extremely successful and felt it was time to move on to new passions. And although she is one of the wisest people I know, she admitted to me that the question, "Who will I be if I'm not the businesswoman?" had crept into her mind many times. The truth is, we become so identified with our roles that we feel lost without them. We're often frightened of the unknown and of not having something to identify with. That's why you'll even meet retired people who will say, "Hi, I'm George—I'm a former businessman." The attachment to the role is so deep that it's difficult to let go of, even when it no longer exists.

It's very freeing to see yourself as a person first and as a role second. For example, I see myself as Richard, a person, a spiritual being, first. And one of the things I do is write books. That's one of my roles as I try to fulfill what I believe is one of my purposes in life. That's very different, however, from seeing myself as "Richard the author," which would mean that if I weren't writing books, I'd be lost.

From my perspective, the goal is to perform your roles as impeccably as possible—do the best you can, and be all you can be—but never lose sight of the fact that you are not the role. That way, the role can come and go—you will have successes and failures, highs and lows, and all the rest—and you'll still be okay.

This is both a philosophical as well as a practical strategy to contemplate. Often, when I speak to men about this issue, they feel relieved, almost as though a weight has been taken off their backs. One man said to me, "As I've attempted to keep in mind that I am not my job, I feel less pressure to perform, as if there's less on the line. Ironically, however, I now feel like I'm doing a better job." That same feeling has been true for me, and I suspect it may be for you, as well.

65

WAIT

Many men have the tendency to charge full speed ahead—in our actions, responses, even our thoughts. And there's no question that there are times when this tendency is not only appropriate, but when it also works to our advantage.

There are other times, however, when the opposite is true, times when waiting, if only for a moment or two, can pay huge dividends.

Just the other day, I received a phone call letting me know of a screw-up that was going to create major havoc in my schedule. My initial impulse was to pick up the phone immediately and chew someone out. I've learned, however, that it's often best to wait. In this particular instance, this turned out to be true. Within ten minutes, I received an apologetic phone call saying there was not a problem, after all. Rather than compound the problem, making the people involved even more tense and defensive, the act of waiting proved to be an adequate solution.

Our impulse to take action can greatly interfere with our own wisdom. I was at a conference when a man nervously shared his concern over a pending problem. The man next to me suggested to him that if he would be patient and have faith, the answer would occur to him. On the surface, it seemed like superficial advice or like the man was simply trying to be supportive. But the reality is, his advice was much more than that.

After lunch, the man with the concern confirmed that, sure enough, an answer had come to him suddenly, during lunch, when he was all alone with nothing on his mind. By pulling back from his thoughts and waiting, his wisdom had been given the chance to simmer—without too much conscious effort. It's ironic, especially to me, but often our most effective thinking and our best ideas come, not when we are forcing thoughts or ideas, but instead when we choose to wait. Doing so allows our thoughts to percolate and to surface, almost like it's happening independently. To be sure, it doesn't always happen on demand or conveniently over lunch. However, it is an effective alternative to attempting to force ideas to develop.

It can be tricky to wait and be patient because it so often goes against our natural impulses. However, if you give it a fair try, you may find yourself feeling less reactive—and a whole lot more peaceful—right away. And as an added bonus, you may find yourself coming up with some pretty great ideas.

66

HAVE A CHANGE OF HEART

Here's an effective way to find some peace in your life. Think of something you've struggled with for a long time, something you're really stubborn about that tends to be a source of irritation or frustration. Now imagine what could happen if you were somehow able to make peace with it, to see it differently, whatever "it" happens to be.

We all have things we struggle with, aspects of our lives that seem to create ongoing stress. Perhaps it's a relationship, a nagging fear or anxiety, or a habit of some kind that gets in your way.

Suppose you have a conflict with someone you work with. For several years you've "put up" with him. You avoid contact whenever possible and have silent conversations in your mind about how much you dislike him. Each time you see him or even think of him, you cringe.

The question is, What's in it for you to continue your inner strife? You may have all sorts of good reasons for your feelings, but the truth is, they are of no value to you.

You could, of course, hope that he changes or loses his job. But then again, that's probably out of your control and most likely won't happen. The other possibility is that your enemy will change his ways and will come to you with a sincere apology, and a well-thought-out plan for an ongoing truce. Unfortunately, that's probably even less likely than his early departure from his job.

The good and bad news is that there is really only one legitimate alternative, and that is to have a change of heart. I say it's bad news, because it's all up to you; you have to be the one to change. Yet it's actually good news, because it's totally within your power to do so.

A change of heart is much more than a four-word pep talk or something that looks good in a book on happier living. It's actually a very practical way to reduce sources of angst and stress in your life. By having a change of heart, you make the decision to see something in a new light, to shift what has probably become a knee-jerk reaction or an ingrained way of thinking.

A man once told me that for most of his life, he saw others as underachievers. He said that his change of heart involved seeing his own arrogance and realizing that people have vastly differing sets of expectations. He told me that he now realized that his need to achieve had a lot to do with his own compulsions and obsessions. The result of his change of heart was that he now sees people as people instead of dividing them into achievers and nonachievers. This is a much nicer way to experience life.

You may tend to see people as competition, or as adversaries. If so, a change of heart might involve learning to see the innocence in them. Or you might see life as a contest, but wish to stop keeping score so much of the time. In this case, having a change of heart might mean redefining what it means to be successful. There are countless ways that a change of heart could be helpful.

Sometimes, a change of heart can come about by one's own quiet reflection. The awareness of the need for a change of heart, along with the desire, is all it takes. Other times, a close friend or even a counselor can be of great service. He or she can help you see your own blind spots or assist you in identifying new ways to look at life.

However you do it, it's well worth the effort. I've had a number of changes of heart over my lifetime. Each time, I've looked back and wondered how I could have seen things the way that I did. I hope you'll reflect on this idea, and, if it's appropriate and you feel it would be helpful, have a change of heart of your own.

67

HONOR THE HUMILITY FACTOR

I had a dispute over a charge for something that I had purchased. I was told it would be "x," but the bill reflected "y." My guess is that most people have had a similar experience at one time or another. If you have, you know that it can be a bit frustrating.

I called the gentleman who took the order, and was amazed at his reaction. Not only did he take full responsibility, but he did so in a nondefensive, friendly way. He apologized in a sincere manner and took care of the problem immediately. I was so impressed that, despite the error, I couldn't wait to do business with him again.

Looking back over the years, it's clear to me that the greatest frustrations I've had with people had to do, not so much with mistakes, but with the response to the mistakes. If someone is reactive, defensive, difficult, and blaming—it makes dealing with him or her a big hassle. If they can't admit (or even see) their contribution to a problem or issue, it seems to compound the problem and makes dealing with it that much more frustrating.

Without knowing it, people who lack humility create enormous stress for themselves. Rather than having the support, trust, admiration, and encouragement of others, the opposite tends to occur. People are usually mad and frustrated with them, which creates all sorts of problems.

This dynamic has certainly been true for me. I've made tons of mistakes in my life. When I've had humility—toward the people I work with, my friends, family, spouse, children, and others—those mistakes are usually forgiven and I'm able to move on. On the other hand, when I've dug my heels in, become stubborn, and lacked humility, the problems were exacerbated. The people involved ended up even more mad and frustrated at me—maybe even disgusted. The lesson for me has been clear: Everyone wins when you act with humility, which involves, among other things, the willingness to look at your own contribution to problems and to see other points of view, as well as the willingness to apologize.

Obviously, for humility to be effective, it must be genuine. In some ways, false humility can be worse than a lack of humility. When humility is expressed to manipulate someone or to make it appear as though someone is sorry, it can (and probably should) backfire.

One of the ways to create more humility in your heart is to reinforce its value. If you reflect on the subject, you'll probably think of many instances where humility has touched your life and where a lack of humility has made you cringe. If you've experienced genuine humility in your own life, you've already seen its gentle power in action. You've seen how well people respond to humility with respect, forgiveness, and grace.

I sometimes imagine how wonderful the world could be if each of us in our own small way would become slightly more humble. Let's work together to make that happen.

68

ACKNOWLEDGE YOUR
INNER INTELLIGENCE

I'd like to differentiate, for a moment, between your intelligence and your inner intelligence. Most of us enjoy or at least have no problem acknowledging how smart we are (for example, at figuring things out with our intellect). Few men, however (at least that I've spoken to), seem to acknowledge an even deeper intelligence that exists within all of us.

Our inner intelligence, when trusted, is a great source of comfort. Some people refer to inner intelligence as wisdom. Whatever you call it, it's that part of us that knows what to do. But it knows what to do, not because you've racked your brain about it, but because you've allowed an answer to come to you.

As men, we often pride ourselves on our ability to plow through things. We like to think that we can do it, so we rely on hard work, perseverance, and effort. And the good news is, very often that's a great asset that works well.

On the other hand, there are times when we would be better served by backing off or by not trying so hard. The truth is, there are times when we don't have an answer or we don't know what to do. Other times, we are pondering a question of the heart—something that requires not intelligence in the traditional sense, but wisdom.

Suppose, for example, that you need to have a discussion with your teenager about the dangers of drug use or to talk to your wife about a concern you are having. Or you need to look at an old problem in a new way. There are many times when cookie-cutter answers don't fit or when turning to experts or common knowledge won't work. Usually, these times are related to matters of the heart. They are issues that require a deeper type of intelligence.

Wisdom transcends traditional intelligence. Instead of surfacing when we fill our mind with data, information, and plans of action, it shows up in the absence of these things. In other words, instead of thinking about an answer, we actually stop thinking (or trying to think) of an answer. We consciously empty our mind, which has the effect of allowing this other, more unconscious form of thought to unfold. We simply trust that the answer is in there, even if it's not immediately apparent.

On the surface, this might sound a little weird because it's more difficult to quantify this type of intelligence. While it's not as visible as traditional intelligence, I can assure you that it's anything but weird. To the contrary, it's a powerful and extremely effective way to approach life. The answers that you receive will delight and perhaps even surprise you. You'll find yourself saying things like, "Wow, where did that come from?"

Knowing that you have this type of intelligence within you is very reassuring because it lets you off the hook. Instead of panicking when you don't have an answer or pretending that you do—you'll feel more peaceful knowing that if you quiet down and wait, you'll find an answer just around the corner. By experimenting with this other type of intelligence, your life will become richer and more peaceful.

69

USE HINDSIGHT TO
CREATE FORESIGHT

The first time I heard the expression, "Everything is easy with the benefit of hindsight," I sort of brushed it off, thinking it was somewhat obvious. After all, it's true. If you knew, in advance, what a certain result was going to be, you could alter your behavior and produce a better result.

At some point, I began thinking about the broader implications of this wisdom. What I've discovered is that we have the benefit of hindsight in our lives a great deal of the time. The only problem is, we fail to use it very often.

I once heard a good definition of insanity—when you keep doing the exact same thing and expect a different result. In a nutshell, that's what hindsight is all about: to keep you from doing the same things and expecting different results.

An acquaintance of mine told me that he was dreading the upcoming holidays. He was going to be visiting his in-laws with his wife and kids. When I asked him about his concerns, he said, "It's always the same. It drives me crazy to be in such close quarters. There's too much togetherness and not enough space. We all drive each other nuts after a few days."

I asked him if he had ever considered renting a hotel room close by. That way, there could be plenty of togetherness, but he could control how much, at least to some degree. Immediately, he launched into three or four reasons why "the family didn't do it that way" and how poorly that decision would be received.

He has the benefit of hindsight at his disposal. He knows, with a good degree of probability, what the outcome is going to be. He knows, in advance, how he is going to feel. He has experienced it many times. But his resistance to using his hindsight to create foresight—and a possible solution—pretty much guarantees that he will have yet another stressful experience.

It's an interesting challenge to know where something is probably headed and to find balance between taking precautions to avoid the usual stress and being open-minded enough to effect change. Personally, I think the best way to resolve this challenge is to strike a balance between the two. For instance, the man headed home for the holidays might go ahead and book the hotel room, but also make the commitment to himself that he absolutely won't be looking for problems that aren't really there. He can make a concerted effort to make this year the best family visit ever— but still have the hotel room, just in case.

Often we make assumptions about things that are mostly in our imaginations. We made plans, for example, to visit some good friends who lived about five hours away. Our friends had offered that we should stay in their home, but something was telling me it might be more comfortable to stay in a hotel. Hindsight was reminding me that, in the past, with other friends, a bit more space would have been nice. Like my friend visiting his in-laws, I imagined it might hurt their feelings, but decided to bring it up gently.

It turned out they were totally relieved and were thinking the very same thing. Six kids and four adults in anyone's home would take a toll. We were all on the same page, but no one had really wanted to bring it up for fear of rocking the boat. I'm sure having the extra space was one of the reasons we had one of the best weekends ever. Great friends, great times, plenty of togetherness, as well as plenty of spacc.

The benefit of hindsight can help us in many aspects of our lives. It can help us predict and prevent problems. It can also help us make adjustments and changes that can make our lives easier and less stressful. If someone is distrustful or dishonest nine times in a row, that tells us something. If we approach a problem a certain way and have never had satisfactory results, it might be time to try a new approach. Whether you're dealing with personal or professional issues, using hindsight is one of the best ways I know of to minimize and reduce stress in an otherwise stressful world.

70

DIVERSIFY

Often, when we think of the word "diversify," we associate it with an investment strategy. To diversify your portfolio means to spread your risk and, in some cases, enhance your potential. Most people seem to think it's a wise thing to do.

It's interesting, however, how seldom we work on diversifying the rest of our lives. Men are notorious for believing in focus and being single-minded. And certainly there's a place for this attitude in our lives. On the other hand, taken to an extreme, a nondiverse life would become very boring, not only to yourself, but to those around you, as well.

Imagine that your only interest in life was in widgets; that was all you thought about, cared about, and talked about, all day, every day. While most of us aren't quite that bad, we can, if we're not careful, move in that direction.

To diversify your life doesn't mean that you lose focus or become scattered. Instead, it simply means you become more open to and interested in new areas of life (and far more interesting to others, as well). Personally, I've found that being more open and diverse has reduced my feelings of stress because it has helped me reinforce the fact that life is so much bigger than the things I sometimes worry about.

Diversifying your life doesn't have to be a big deal. It might mean starting to read a book on a new subject occasionally or taking a class just for fun rather than "to improve" yourself. It could involve spending time with new people, becoming involved in a new cause, or engaging in a new activity.

One day I picked up a book on whales and read the entire thing, cover to cover, without putting it down. I didn't know the first thing about whales before reading the book, but I found it absolutely fascinating. Since that time, I've learned a little about the ocean and have spent more time near it. I love it. It's no big deal, but my new interest has certainly added to my life in many unexpected ways.

I've met men who, quite out of the blue, happened upon a new passion or cause, simply because they were willing to explore something new. They may have been willing to go to a meeting or listen to someone's story or join new friends for dinner, or whatever. However it happened, being willing to diversify opened the door for something new to occur. Their own lives, and the world as a whole, are better off because of it.

So open your mind and experiment with something new. You may be surprised at the wonders that will present themselves.

71

CALCULATE THE NUMBER OF
THINGS THAT WENT RIGHT TODAY

The first time I suggested to someone that they give this a try, I was half kidding. He was complaining about this and that, and I asked him to pull out a piece of paper and do some calculations. To my surprise, he took my suggestion to heart. In a matter of less than a minute, he smiled, put his piece of paper down, and said he got the point.

Among the first few items on his list were these: "I woke up healthy. The kids were at school on time, homework done. Likewise, I was at work with plenty of time to spare. A huge number of phone calls were returned and my projects were going fine. My wife got home safely from her trip to the other side of the country." In addition, he included the fact that he had had a nice lunch with three coworkers and that all arrived on time, safely, coming from different locations. In addition, there no computer crashes in the office.

It's easy to see that he was playing along with me, but the more I've asked people to experiment with this idea, the more people have thanked me for bringing it to their attention. In a way, when you stop to think about it, it's awesome. I recently spoke to a group of people and raised the question, How many things had to go right in order that all of us could be here together today? There was a definite stillness in the room as people reflected.

The truth is, while most of us complain about the things that go wrong, the vast majority of things go right. In fact, the number of things that went right today, all over the world, is miraculous. Think about computers and transportation. How about telephones and fax machines, as well as other, more sophisticated technology? What about food distribution and food safety, heating and air conditioning? Then there are scheduling and communicating—traffic flow, deliveries, and the like. Alarm clocks went off on time; people did what they said they would. I could go on and on for pages, as could you.

Occasionally, someone will accuse me of being overly optimistic. Believe it or not, this isn't really true. I know there are enormous problems to deal with, hardships, and things that go wrong. Like you, I'm doing what I can to help. I also experience hassles, delays, canceled flights, difficult people, things that don't work out, negotiation disputes, issues with my kids, neighbors, and so forth. But I also understand that the problems pale in comparison to the number of things that go right.

When you think about "news," you're usually thinking about bad news. A friend who works in a newsroom once told me, "It isn't news unless it's bad news." There are certainly exceptions, but generally speaking, he was correct. You'd never read the headline, "It was an amazing day—10,000 planes arrived safely, without incident, at their destinations." Instead, the headline will always be about the one accident that did occur.

We tend to treat our personal life stories in much the same way. We may have one hundred little things going on in our lives that we completely take for granted, even though they are blessings. But what we focus on and talk about with others are the one or two irritating things that are happening.

My goal isn't to turn anyone into a Pollyanna or an unrealistically happy person. It's simply to remind people that, hey, we're pretty darn lucky to be here and to have so many things going smoothly. Spending a little time calculating the number of things that go right is a simple but powerful way to reactivate our sense of wonder and gratitude. I hope you'll spend a little time doing the math.

72

UNDERREACT

Most men have probably heard of "overreaction" and most of us do just that, sometimes many times a day. Yet my guess is that most of us feel that to do so isn't a good thing. When we overreact, we are blowing something out of proportion, making it into a big deal, and sweating the small stuff.

Despite the overwhelming distaste for overreactions, few people that I've spoken to have ever considered the far more peaceful alternative—to underreact. Once they have tried it, however, many are hooked on the idea.

Suppose you are delivered some potentially stressful news—for instance, there is a problem at work. Let's compare two scenarios. In the first scenario, you overreact. You flip out, lose your cool, and get stressed. Your colleagues sense your frustration and feed off it, like fuel to a fire. The room begins to fill with worry and stress.

In the second scenario, however, you respond more peacefully. You underreact to what is taking place. Instead of having a knee-jerk, negative reaction, assuming the worst and getting all worked up, you keep your cool and work on the assumption that an answer is just around the corner. Your feathers aren't rumpled, even slightly. Your calm nature is reassuring to everyone, and the feeling in the room is confident and friendly.

Sounds good in theory, but how do you do it? The way I see it is this: Reactions are usually nothing more than habits we get into. Something happens, and we are accustomed to reacting in a certain way—as though there isn't enough time or as if it's necessary to be stressed. But later, after the fact, we are able to look back and see that a vast majority of the time, it wasn't at all necessary to overreact. In retrospect, we can see that had we remained calm, we would have solved the problem anyway. The difference would have been that we could have avoided most of the stress, conflict, and agitation associated with whatever it was we had to deal with. The trick is to bring that after-the-fact wisdom to the present. In other words, to be confident that everything is going to be okay—while it's happening.

Here's a simple example. You're on your way to an important meeting and you're stuck in horrible, unexpected traffic. Immediately, you assume the worst. Your shoulders get tense, and you start anticipating having to explain yourself. You think of excuses, and you start to criticize yourself for not giving yourself more time. How many times has something like that happened to you?

Now be honest. Out of all the times that you've been running late, how many of those times did you somehow manage to make it? How many times were you no more than a few minutes late and it turned out not to matter very much? Or, as is often the case, the person you were meeting was understanding and forgiving. It's a wild guess, but I'd estimate that out of every twenty times we flip out, nineteen of those times it was totally unnecessary. And even in the one exception, stressing out didn't help solve the problem.

Believe me, I'm not suggesting you ever run late on purpose. To the contrary, I'm a huge advocate of giving yourself extra time. On the other hand, when you reflect on the way things usually turn out, it's easy to see that not always, but often, we make a big deal out of nothing. In other words, when we're running late, we could just as easily relax and resolve to get to where we're going as quickly as we can in the circumstances. We can make a mental note to leave earlier next time—and then let it go. It's not as if gripping the wheel, swearing, or assuming the worst is going to make the car go any faster.

Part of the problem with an overreaction is that it rarely seems like an overreaction. Instead, it seems like an appropriate and necessary response to something that is happening. It's usually only after the fact that someone can look back and admit that a reaction was disproportionate to what was occurring.

A similar illusion can occur when you first make the decision to underreact. It can seem as if you should be acting more crazy, as though a more dramatic response is necessary. Once you get used to it, however, you'll see that an underreaction is often the most appropriate one, as was true in our driving example above. Far from being superficial, apathetic, or unresponsive, an underreaction is often the perfect response. It's a response filled with patience, wisdom, and peace. It allows you the wherewithal to solve whatever issues present themselves. If you keep your cool, then when you get to your appointment, even a few minutes late, you'll be composed and ready to go. You won't have wasted any energy fretting over something you had no control over.

Underreactions work beautifully at work and at home. If you have a spouse and children, it can come in handy virtually every day. I know that when I keep my cool, I solve problems in about one-tenth as much time as I do when I lose my bearings. When you get used to responding in a more level-headed, calm manner to the small stuff of your day, you'll find that most things will work themselves out pretty easily. And if something isn't working out, you always have the option of turning up the heat.

I encourage you to give this new type of response a shot. Start with really small stuff and work your way up. My guess is that you'll find it a lot easier than you think, and that, in time, you will have no interest in going back to overreacting.

73

LET GO OF THE PAST

I was talking to a gentleman who was complaining about the way he was raised by his parents. He told me about three separate incidents that happened more than thirty years ago.

His frustration reminded me of a very important spiritual principle: We are not upset by events of the past. Instead, we are upset because of the attention we are giving to those past events—here, in the present.

It's interesting to consider that if the events themselves were the culprits, then we'd all be bent out of shape—all of the time. Think about the millions of negative events that have occurred throughout history, including all the painful things that may have occurred to you. Yet, despite the negativity, here we are—in one piece. It's only when our attention drifts to those past events—we focus on them and take our thoughts to heart—that we have a problem. It's so easy to become absorbed in (or worse yet, riveted to) our memories, almost as if the events are happening all over again.

Seeing our past as memory—as thoughts carried through time (nothing more or less)—is an extremely powerful insight. It allows you to have perspective and forgiveness, and to let things go as they come up. Without this insight, life can be (and usually is) quite difficult, because as painful memories come up—which they do for all of us—there will be a tendency to relate to those thoughts and memories as if they were real or happening all over again. On the other hand, when you relate to the thoughts of your past as mere thoughts, it's far easier to dismiss them or at least give them less significance.

Someone shared with me the following story, which, I believe, is a perfect illustration of this idea: He was working on a big project that was almost complete. It had been a major hassle and a ton of work, but he was just about there. Some thoughts began to drift through his mind about a previous employer who never would have had the confidence in him to do this particular job. He remembered how it felt to work for someone who didn't believe in him, and he started to feel a little resentful and smug. One thought led to another, and another—until he was actually getting angry.

Then it happened. He woke up to the fact that he was right in the middle of an all-out thought attack about his past. He said it was the strangest thing—his thinking seemed absolutely "real," but in that instant, he remembered that it was only a memory, a thought that seemed real.

He was now free to enjoy his new accomplishment instead of wallowing in resentful thoughts from his past. I think the rest of us (myself included) can learn a great deal from his experience. We all have events from our past that haunt us as they reemerge as thoughts disguised as the real thing. Keep in mind the idea that thoughts can't hurt us without our consent.

74

ANTICIPATE DEFENSIVENESS

Some things in life are difficult, if not impossible to predict. Guessing how long you're going to live, for example, or whether or not you're going to get sick certainly fall into this category. Or, on a lighter note, it's difficult to predict specifically how well your favorite sports team is going to do before the season begins. On the other hand, some other things are fairly easy to predict. Luckily, figuring out what is likely to create a defensive reaction is in this latter group.

Learning to anticipate defensiveness is an extremely effective way to make your life a whole lot easier. Dealing with defensive people and defensive reactions is difficult and often stressful. When people are defensive, they are at their worst. They become angry, adversarial, irrational, and hostile. Plus, after the fact, you're forced to deal with it in some way—making adjustments, fighting back, walking on eggshells, or just plain walking away.

However, when you can anticipate a defensive reaction before it happens, you can make subtle adjustments in the way you deal with people. Having the wisdom to anticipate defensive reactions allows you to avoid a great deal of conflict in the first place by not pushing certain buttons in people and by not engaging in certain types of communication and behavior that are likely to set someone off. The payoff to you is that each conflict you prevent is one less hassle and source of stress you have to deal with. This saves you time, energy, aggravation, and stress.

There are several major ways we increase the likelihood of a defensive response. Here are a few to think about. I've found that being aware of them helps us avoid them in the first place by encouraging us to make small adjustments. They are: 1) threatening someone in any way; 2) not allowing someone to "save face"; 3) putting someone on the spot, especially in front of others; and 4) leaving someone an angry voice- or e-mail.

What all these tendencies have in common is that they entail backing someone into a corner or applying pressure. They leave a person very few options other than to feel or act defensive. While it's certainly not our responsibility to keep someone from feeling defensive (that's their own job), it is nevertheless in our own best interest to keep from pushing someone else's buttons if we have any legitimate options. And not always, but most of the time, there are options.

For example, suppose you're at work and a mistake is made. In your mind, you've already placed blame, and your initial reaction is to confront that person. That's certainly your choice to make. Yet, in situations like this, you're at a fork in the road. You can bring it up now, as is your impulse, in front of others, perhaps in order to set an example of the behavior you expect. Or you can wait a little while until you've cooled off and have an opportunity to speak to the person in private. Obviously, specifics will play an important part in dictating your behavior. But, all things being equal, you might be better off waiting a while. To confront the person right away will probably create a defensive response.

The same can be said about sending off an angry e-mail or leaving an irritated voice message. As obnoxious as someone might have been, and as mad as you may be (regardless of how justified the anger or frustration), it's always a good idea to ask yourself the question, "What is the probable result of this voice- or e-mail going to be?" By taking a step back, reflecting for a minute and asking the right questions, you might very well decide that to send it is not worth the trade-off. Remember, you'll probably feel much less reactive if you wait a while. If you still wish to have the confrontation, you can always do so at a later time.

Often, when we put someone on the spot, forcing them to react instantly, or to make an instant decision, we risk making them feel pressured. If possible, try to allow people a chance to think about things or give them a way out before requiring a response. Recently, for example, someone said to me over the phone, "I'll be in town the week of the tenth, and would love to stay with you. Is that all right?" Even something that simple and innocent put me on the spot. I would have appreciated it very much had the person instead put it like this: "I'll be around the week of the tenth, and I'd love to see you if you're free. Could you check your schedule, think about it, and let me know sometime in the next week or so?" It's essentially the same request, but with a less pressured feeling.

Whether you're at home with your wife, sharing with friends, making a request, or tackling a problem, learning to anticipate defensive reactions is a helpful skill to develop. It's one of those skills whereby a little time and reflection now can pay off big-time as a stress prevention tool for years to come.

75

THINK, "YEAH, SO?"

A few years back I was sitting with a man who taught me an invaluable lesson about life. I was complaining about several little things that weren't quite right. I was feeling hassled and bothered by my professional, as well as my personal life. I remember making statements like, "And he didn't call me back," and "My friend said this." I must have been in a really bad mood.

The person I was with had been giving me his full attention, but began to appear a bit puzzled, as if he didn't understand the implications or seriousness of what I had been saying. So I continued. "Don't you understand—he didn't even give me the courtesy of a return call." Looking back, it's obvious that I was venting and wanted his commiseration.

I remember his response because it hit me like a ton of bricks. In a respectful yet curious tone, he simply said, "Yeah, so?," as if he were waiting for the punchline. He honestly didn't "get it."

The "Yeah, so?" lesson was a variation of another lesson I had learned years earlier. Once, when I was a very young man, I was quite mad about something that had happened to me. The adult friend who was with me made the statement, "I can see why you're mad," but then followed up with a question, "Why so mad?" The emphasis was on the "so."

Both of these instances encouraged me to start asking some important questions that assist me to this day. For example, Why must I become bummed out simply because an event of the day didn't meet my expectations? Why *so* mad?

How often do we assume, without question, that we must respond to something in a certain way? For example, is it absolutely necessary that we become defensive when someone criticizes us? Is it mandatory that we become frustrated when traffic is heavy? Must we become angry when someone disagrees with us or simply because we have to deal with a hassle? And if so, why *so* angry? Who made up these cause-and-effect relationships anyway?

These are interesting questions to ponder. In no way am I suggesting that it's bad, or wrong, to have these reactions. I'm only asking the question, Are they carved in stone?

What I've come to believe is that they are not. We have a choice in the matter.

Step back for a moment, and see if you don't agree. Someone doesn't call you back, or the weather changes and spoils your plans, or your kid catches a cold at an inconvenient time, or your wife or girlfriend says the wrong thing. In these and other instances, you certainly have "the right" to become upset and bothered; in fact, most people probably would. But you have another option as well. You could shrug it off and say to yourself, "Yeah, so?" as if to say, "Simply more evidence that life doesn't always accommodate us with our preferred outcomes." Or if you can't help but get mad, maybe you don't have to get *so* mad.

Personally, I find this more accepting and lighthearted response to events and hassles quite refreshing. It has helped to reinforce my belief that it's not as necessary to sweat the small stuff as many of us tend to think it is.

76

TRY NOT TO BE FRUSTRATED
WHEN IT MIGHT BE MORE
APPROPRIATE TO BE GRATEFUL

I'm writing this strategy while sitting at a parking gate at Chicago's O'Hare International Airport. I'm supposed to be on my way back to San Francisco tonight to be sure I'm on time for my daughter's birthday. This trip is a little different from many of the others I've taken, in that we'd already taxied out to the runway and were waiting for our turn to take off.

After a considerable wait, however, the captain came on over the loudspeaker and said, "Sorry folks, we are going to have to taxi back to the gate and fix a mechanical problem." So we waited some more, and the plane eventually turned around to look for an open gate—of which there were none. So we waited some more.

Eventually, after what seemed like a very long time, we arrived back at a suitable gate. And here I sit, at this moment. The mechanics have come aboard and are doing their best to fix the problem, which appears to be of a nonserious nature.

Here's the interesting part. While a few of the passengers seem okay with what's going on, the vast majority seem to be sweating it big time. There are moans and groans of frustration and disapproval, mixed with a bit of whining and complaining. People (mostly men) feel put out and inconvenienced—despite the fact that well-trained professionals may have just saved their life. The price: a two-hour delay. Seems like a pretty good trade-off to me. It's not that there's no merit to the complaints—everyone would rather be on time than late—it's just that the advantages far outweigh the disadvantages.

I couldn't feel more grateful. It's amazing to me that we have such talented people, as well as the technology that can spot troubles like this—before they become serious. It seems to me that to be annoyed at this issue is selfish and shortsighted. After all, these experts have dedicated their careers to ensure our safety. Thank god for them.

There are many examples in life where we become frustrated, when, with the benefit of a little perspective, we'd probably feel grateful instead. Someone gives us some advice, for example, and we act or feel defensive. But remember, the advice may help us prevent or solve certain problems. And, even if it doesn't, it's quite possible that the advice was given not as a slap, but from concern, love, or a desire to help.

Other times, a minor problem develops at home or at work. We immediately become really frustrated, often failing to see the hidden gifts in the situation. Becoming aware of a relatively minor problem can very often help us to make adjustments that will prevent far more serious problems down the road.

Just the other day, for example, I was talking to a man who was involved in a very minor accident. While no one was hurt, his car had a few hundred dollars' worth of damage. He was very upset because there was some problem with his insurance. It turned out, however, to be a huge blessing, since he became aware that he was vastly underinsured in other areas. Had the minor accident not happened, he may have never become aware of his much larger potential exposure—until it was too late.

I'm not advocating becoming a Pollyanna about hassles, because I don't like them any more than anyone else. On the other hand, there are many times in our lives when things appear on the surface to be problems—but, in fact, they very well may be tremendous gifts. Looking for those gifts instead of focusing only on the problem eases our minds and makes life a little better.

77

CONSIDER THAT "NEEDING A VACATION" MAY NOT BE THE REAL PROBLEM

I've heard the words "I need a vacation" so many times. And certainly there are times when we really do need one. We need to get away from our normal routine and do something totally different.

On the other hand, it's easy to convince ourselves that a simple vacation, a few days or a week away from our hectic routine, will ease the stress of our crazy lives—when the real problem is that our lives have become crazy. If that's the case, needing a vacation may not be the real problem—and taking one may not be the best solution.

Becoming overwhelmed doesn't happen overnight. Instead, it sneaks up on us. A few commitments and obligations turn into dozens. There is a funny but powerful saying regarding military defense spending: A billion here, a billion there; pretty soon it adds up to some big money. A similar perspective can be used in our own lives. Many of our commitments may not seem huge when seen in isolation; some in fact, may take only a few minutes to fulfill. However, combined, they can really add up.

There's an easy comparison on the subject of clutter. Have you ever stopped to think about how much stuff we collect? Much of it we don't even want. Mail, for example, pours into our homes to the tune of at least twenty pieces a day. Do you know that if you allowed twenty pieces of mail to come into your home each day for a month and didn't throw any of it away, at the end of the month you'd have almost 500 pieces of mail piled up? In a year, that number would soar to more than 5,000. And that's just mail.

It's the same with our lives. Many of us work forty, fifty, sixty, even seventy hours a week. Plus, we have important relationships, including children to love and care for. We have a home and perhaps a yard to take care of and projects to pursue. We may have pets. Many of us would like to squeeze in some exercise, maybe even a hobby or two. We have social responsibilities and are on various committees. We attend church or temple, and pursue other spiritual or religious disciplines, and in addition, we may volunteer our time.

If you keep adding things to your list—when you're already maxed out—at some point you'll go nuts; your circuits will burst. It's a wonder we do as well as we do.

I've found that reducing my commitment level has been far more beneficial than any vacation I've ever taken. Vacations, after all, last only a week or two. But reducing commitments and learning to say no is helpful 365 days a year.

The first step in finding a solution is identifying the problem. Take an honest look at your life and the number of activities you are involved with. If a vacation is appropriate, take it and have a great time. In addition, however, why not consider the possibility that needing a vacation may not be the real problem? An adjustment in lifestyle might be the real solution. This simple realization may help you bring the sanity back to your life. It did for me.

78

AVOID THE "CAUGHT UP" TRAP

Imagine a poor little fly caught up in a spiderweb. Dazed and confused, he struggles until the end.

Sadly, there are times when our minds are like that helpless little fly. We get completely caught up in our own thoughts. And when we do, boy, do we struggle.

Men are able to get caught up about practically anything—the size of our bank account or the speed of our computer. We fret about our schedules, what other people think, or a dent in the car. We get caught up about our past or the future. Sometimes, it's about something someone said to us or about us. We get bent out of shape by many things—our thoughts about our partner's ex-boyfriend, politics, or something in the news. Sometimes it's deep stuff, but often it's fairly superficial. You name it, one of us will be caught up about it.

Being caught up is like obsessing about something. It's that familiar feeling of stewing in our minds, sweating it, going over and over something, again and again. We think about it, analyze it, churn it about, and so forth. It can go on for a long time.

When you think about sweating the small stuff, what you're really doing is getting caught up about something. Something happens (or doesn't happen), and we think about it. Then we think about it some more. Then we do it again. We blow it up bigger than it probably is. Sometimes we can't sleep. Part of us believes that, if we could just think about it a little more, the problem would be solved.

The simple truth is, the fact that you're caught up in your thinking is often more relevant to the stress you're feeling than whatever it is you're caught up about. For example, if you're upset about something someone said about you at work, the fact that you're caught up in it is the reason you're feeling so stressed. Proof of this is that, once you're no longer obsessing about it, you'll be back to feeling fine again. Your stress had little to do with what was said; it had everything to do with your reaction to it. And that's true, across the board, whatever small stuff you're caught up about.

Yet, if you asked one hundred people the question, Why are you so darned upset? I'd guess that a vast majority them would say, "I'm upset because of that person at work" (or whatever). The few exceptions, however, are the people who are able to dismiss those things that aren't worth being upset over.

The trick is to recognize when you're caught up, and you do this by paying attention to the way you're feeling. If you're feeling upset, stressed out, bothered, or agitated, chances are you're simply caught up in your thoughts again. By paying attention to the way you're feeling, you're able to catch yourself, back off, and feel better. It's as if you say, "There I go again." By not making a big deal out of it, yet seeing how your thoughts participate in your negative feelings, you're often able to lighten up.

I encourage you to give this a try. The next time you're feeling a little stressed, see if you can notice yourself becoming caught up in your own thinking. Then, instead of continuing on your train of thought, try to back off a little. Say something to yourself like, "Okay, there I go again," or some other way to remind yourself that the real problem isn't so much what you're upset about, but rather the fact that you're caught up in it to begin with.

There are an unlimited number of things that can potentially upset us. But learning to avoid the "caught up" trap is a pretty easy way to reduce that number to a more manageable amount. The more often you notice yourself becoming engaged in this common trap, and the earlier you catch yourself, the easier it becomes. My guess is you'll benefit from this strategy right away.

79

SEE THE IRONY OF
"STRIVING" FOR BALANCE

I asked a large audience the question, How many of you are striving for more balance in your lives? The room was full of raised hands.

It sounds like a great goal, and in a way it is. Yet, if you reflect on the subject of balance for a moment, you may find that striving for balance actually interferes with becoming balanced.

To begin with, it's helpful to examine what balance means to you. To me, it represents a state of equilibrium, of harmony. It's a peaceful center, often in the midst of chaos. To be balanced is to be content, satisfied, and comfortable with where you are and who you are. The reason I say that striving can interfere with balance is because balance is an inner feeling, whereas striving is an external activity.

When you are striving for something—a goal, achievement, success, or whatever else—it means you are, to one degree or another, dissatisfied. In fact, that's why you're striving. You're narrowly focused on the object of your striving. You want something to be different. You want more of something. You're reaching, grasping, and focused on the future. Striving suggests a physical and emotional effort of some kind. It's fair to say that when you strive, you're off-balance.

So in a way, while you can strive for all sorts of things, you can't really strive for balance—you can only become (or be) it. The act of striving—the effort involved—can actually take you away from balance.

This is an important distinction to ponder because, if you're not at least aware of the dichotomy, you may find yourself interfering with the very thing you're trying to create. You'll find yourself trying hard, but going around in circles.

If we feel scattered, frenetic, hurried, and frazzled (out of balance) on the inside, there's no way to organize our lives in a way that really works. A frazzled person who is constantly in a rush will find any number of ways to fill up any free time he does manage to create, with activities—work and otherwise—that will cause additional chaos. It's easy to think that your life would be more balanced if you were able to save more money, or add a hobby, or squeeze in more vacations, or find a new partner, or move to a new city, or whatever. But you're doing these things from an emotional and spiritual place of being rushed, instead of from a place of peace. Therefore, your new schedule or hobbies will, in the end, be treated more as "things to take care of" instead of things that bring balance to your life.

When we feel balanced on the inside, however, we make decisions that reinforce that feeling. We tend to prioritize more effectively and to do those things that really do matter to us. For example, if we feel peaceful and balanced, we find ways to adjust our schedules so that our lives are experienced at a sane pace. We schedule time for ourselves, our families, and anything else that is important to us.

The solution is twofold. First, we want to be sure not to put the cart before the horse. We have to come to the conclusion that balance does indeed stem from the inside, and not from the way we set up our schedules or our lives. In other words, balance comes first—a peaceful life comes out of that balance.

And second, we will want to create more presence in our lives, which translates into balance. Presence involves, for example, being able to do one thing at a time or being able to sit with someone without wishing you were somewhere else. It means being able to fully enjoy what you are doing right now, while you're doing it—rather than doing something so that you'll be able to enjoy it "someday." To have presence means that you recognize it when your mind is racing forward to the next thing while you're still here doing something else.

More often than not, achieving balance involves removing things from our schedules more than it does adding things. The act of taking things away creates the space—physically and emotionally—to rethink and reprioritize.

None of this is to say that you shouldn't constantly be looking for ways to improve your life, yourself, or to make your life easier or more effective. That's all part of it too. But when your striving interferes with and overshadows your experience of daily living, that's when it's impossible to find that peaceful feeling and satisfying way of living.

By allowing yourself to become balanced, rather than striving to become balanced, you'll be able to enjoy the moments of your life, one after another—while, at the same time, becoming all you can be.

80

CHECK YOUR BLIND SPOTS

Years ago, I was driving with a friend. We were having a great conversation when I switched lanes and, completely by accident, cut someone off. I didn't cause a collision, but I could have. For a moment my friend was shaken and annoyed. He yelled out, "Richard, check your blind spots!"

Ever since that time, I've been far more careful. In addition, I've learned that the idea of checking the "blind spots" of my life every once in a while is also a very important thing to do. What I mean is, checking in with dear and trusted friends or family to see if they've noticed any ways in which I might be getting in my own way.

Many of us have close friends or associates who know us really well. We probably have the type of relationship with these people that would allow us to ask for their insights about our behavior or attitudes. People who are close to us, who know us very well, are often able to see things in us that we may not be able to see in ourselves. Sometimes (probably most of the time) the advice is low key, but at other times it can be life-changing.

I have a few friends, for example, with whom I get together on a fairly regular basis. I feel very comfortable asking them for any suggestions and guidance. The advice I ask might be personal or professional. I've had friends tell me, "I think you're taking the issue too personally"; "I think you're overreacting and here's why"; or "I think you owe that person an apology." Other types of advice may include the suggestion to get into, or out of, a business venture, or a business or personal relationship. Or a friend might be able to see that I'm in need of some time off or time alone.

I recently met a man who told me that he had asked a good friend of his a similar question. His friend took him to lunch and told him that, over the past few years, he had noticed that when he drank, he would become argumentative and aggressive. The man had tears in his eyes because his friend's honesty made it possible for him to admit to himself, for the first time, that he had developed a drinking problem. He said that without his friend's asked-for advice, he wouldn't be in recovery today.

Sometimes, when I have made this suggestion, men have responded by saying, "I think it would be difficult to have my own friends lecturing me." But remember, it isn't a lecture—it's advice that you've asked for. And because you're the one who asked, any defensive feelings you might have otherwise had will be lessened. It has always seemed to me that when I've been humble enough to ask for feedback, the person I've asked has always been gentle in their delivery.

There's no question that, for me, the advantages in terms of what I have learned about myself from close friends have far exceeded any disadvantages. The insights have had an enormous positive impact on my life. I hope you'll consider asking similar questions of your own good friends because they, too, may have some valuable insights to share.

81

OPEN YOUR HEART
TO COMPASSION

There are many levels of compassion. For the purposes of this strategy, two come to mind. By incorporating them into your life, you will feel more peaceful and satisfied and, at the same time, you will feel more in tune with your world.

First, at a very deep, fundamental level, it's important to see yourself as connected to everyone else here on our planet. We are all human beings, and we're in this together, so to speak. We are part of the human family. Sure, we are all very different and have vastly different circumstances, but the fact remains that we share a common bond.

We are also part of a giant ecosystem. When something is damaged or destroyed—be it a rain forest, an ocean, a river, or whatever—it affects us all. It affects the food we eat, the air we breathe, and the energy of the universe that we all share.

When you step back, slow down, and reflect on the miracle of life, on the gift of being here on this planet for this brief period of time, it's easy to see how connected we really are to everything else.

That being said, how can we not open our compassionate heart and do what we can to alleviate the suffering in the world? When we know that our actions (and inaction) do make a difference, however small they might seem, we can no longer look the other way.

Some of you may have read my favorite quote from Mother Teresa in one of my previous books: "We cannot do great things on this earth. We can only do small things with great love." Her quote is a perfect introduction to the second aspect of compassion—the practical component.

The truth is, we don't have to do "great things" to make a difference, only small things. By taking small steps and actions, our lives can become instruments of love and compassion. We can and will make a difference.

There are so many things we can do on a day-to-day, moment-to-moment basis. We can start with our own homes and communities, by doing what we can to promote kindness and peace. We can make a difference in our work environment and in the classrooms of our kids. We can donate money, ideas, time, and love to the causes near and dear to our hearts.

Every day we are given hundreds of opportunities to practice compassion in action. We can learn to be less reactive and live with more patience. We can smile when others are serious. We can drive our cars more carefully, pick up litter on the streets, recycle, and reduce our consumption. We can resolve conflicts rather than create them, and we can become less judgmental and more inclusive. When someone is aggressive, we can teach them to be more peaceful. Instead of waiting for an example, we can *be* the example.

The more compassion that enters your heart, the happier and more peaceful you will become. By knowing that you are doing your part to create a better world—whatever form that takes—you will fill any void that exists in your life, and you will begin to find the peace you are looking for.

82

LIVE BY THE MOTTO,

"IT IS AS IT IS"

So much of the time when we're sweating or stressing about something, it's because we're resisting something that we have little or no control over—rather than accepting it for what it is. Someone will make a mistake, for example (or we will), or something will be misplaced or broken. It could be that there is a sudden change in plans or a delay.

Rather than accept what is, we get frustrated, acting as if our frustration will somehow resolve or solve the issue—which, of course, it never does. We have conversations in our heads about these things, commiserate with others, struggle, and feel frustrated. In short, we demand that things be other than they are.

Yet despite our inner struggles and our desire for things to be other than they are, the fact remains, they are as they are. One of the greatest sources of inner peace that I'm aware of (and that I try to practice in my own life) is expressed in the motto, "It is as it is." This prescription for peace is a reminder that there are times in life when acceptance is a far wiser option than struggle.

At one level, this is obvious. Suppose a glass of water falls off the table and smashes on the floor. It's obvious that it is as it is. Anyone can see that. After all, there's broken glass and water all over the floor. But admitting that there's broken glass on the floor is quite different from the accepting attitude of being okay with things as they are, simply because that's the way they really are.

The absolute acceptance of events—even or especially when you don't like them—allows you to completely let go of things, including the frustration that so often accompanies such events. When you remind yourself that it is as it is, you acknowledge the fact that the incident is over and there's no need whatsoever to be overly reactive.

Embracing the truth is much wiser, and ultimately more peaceful than wishing things were different or that they didn't happen as they did. This is true, not because you enjoy spilled water, but because you know that to resist the truth is to create certain pain. In other words, the truth is that there is broken glass on the floor. Now what? The more you insist that it's not true or wish that it hadn't happened, the more pain and regret you will experience and create. To become upset is an exercise in futility.

This is an important insight because it applies to virtually any scenario: you lose your keys, you're passed over for the promotion you feel you deserved, your son brings home a poor report card, the neighbor's dog just destroyed your lawn, your girlfriend was flirting with another man, and whatever else. A more accepting attitude has nothing to do with enjoying these and other potential disappointments, wishing them upon yourself, or advocating them. It's merely an acknowledgment of the truth and a reminder that no amount of wishing things were different will make them any different— at least not right now. There is tremendous freedom that can be experienced when we stop exerting effort by insisting things be different.

As you spend time reflecting on this issue (and hopefully practicing this strategy), you'll find that it gets easier to implement. Reminding yourself that life simply "is as it is" will reap huge rewards, increasing the ease and acceptance with which you move through life.

83

DON'T MISS THE FUN!

In our haste to make plans for our lives, we sometimes—even with the best of intentions—miss out on the life we already have.

One of my favorite personal stories, which demonstrates this point so well, occurred a few years back on a beach in Hawaii. Kris and I were with our kids, and were sitting near other two couples who, between them, had a bunch of adorable children.

Because we were sitting pretty close to the other people, it was easy to hear what they were talking about. From the time they sat down in the warm sand until the time they left an hour or two later, they never stopped planning their vacation. In other words, even though they were on vacation, they were forgetting to stop planning long enough to enjoy it—at least it seemed that way. They talked about their plans for later on that day, how much fun it was going to be to watch the sunset, the restaurants they planned to frequent, and the tours they were looking forward to.

"So what?" you might think. And from a certain perspective, you're absolutely right. Their conversation was totally innocent, and they were simply expressing their excitement about upcoming events.

On the other hand, during the course of their conversation, the five little kids had gathered sand, built, and eventually tore down one of the greatest sandcastles ever. They were having so much fun playing and laughing so hard that I wasn't sure they would ever stop. Their laughter was contagious and cute—and between them and my own kids, it was one of those "life doesn't get any better than this" moments.

Sadly, it didn't appear as though any of the four adults witnessed the joy their kids were experiencing. The whole experience came and went while they were talking about how much fun they were going to have. In a way, it was less like they were on vacation and more like they were still only planning it. Sometimes life really is "what's happening while we're busy making other plans."

I heard another similar story that broke my heart. Apparently, the grandfather of a bride was videotaping his granddaughter's wedding. Since he didn't want to miss a moment, he barely looked up from the camera lens the entire time. The whole ceremony and most of the festivities was spent looking through the hole with one eye shut.

The problem was, the camera didn't work! Ouch. Not only did he miss the entire show, but now he had no way to relive what he missed later on, either.

Obviously, there's nothing wrong with parents having their own fun and not feeling the need to witness every moment of their kids' childhood. Likewise, there's certainly nothing wrong with a grandfather wanting to be able to look back on a very special day. Nevertheless, stories like these remind us that the real joys in life are happening right now, right here, in front of us. We shouldn't spend all of our time planning our lives. Instead, it's okay to spend some time enjoying it right now.

84

SEE THINGS FROM A DISTANCE

A few years ago, there was a beautiful song—one of my all-time favorites—that was extremely popular. It was called "From a Distance" and was sung by Bette Midler.

It was a great song, not only for the music, but for the message. It spoke about the wisdom of seeing things from a distance and about how differently things appear when we do so.

Imagine, for example, how silly an argument with your wife or girlfriend would seem when seen from a long distance. How about the fact that someone slightly dented your car in the parking lot and took off without writing you a note. Space, or distance, puts things into a different, wiser perspective. It makes such events seem so much less urgent and pressing. It doesn't mean you don't care about these things, but instead that you don't have to become overly concerned or reactive about them.

Imagine that your fist is a problem. It could be any problem. Clench it right now. Now take your fist right up against your face so that it's practically covering your eyes. Notice that when it's so close to you, it seems really big and significant. Even something pretty small seems much larger than it is.

Now, gradually, pull your fist away from your eyes as far as you can comfortably reach. Notice how much smaller it looks when you create some distance between your problem and yourself.

The song suggested that, from a distance, people get along with one another better and the most serious problems don't seem to exist. It certainly seems that way to me.

Space, or distance, seems to have an effect on problems similar to that of time. Many of us have heard the expression, "Time heals all wounds," and maybe it does. However, enough space seems to do the same thing, even if not much time has transpired. When you get away from a problem (metaphorically), it is easier to place it into better perspective. We can then see it more clearly, with less clouded vision, and it's easier to find what solutions may be needed.

We can take this wisdom and extend it into our daily lives. By imagining that there is distance between ourselves and the things that bother us, we can create a buffer of sorts, some protection to immunize ourselves. As simple as this seems, it really can help.

I was involved in a minor dispute with someone and found myself really caught up and involved in what sure seemed like a drama. Then I remembered the words, "from a distance," and imagined some space—lots of it—between myself and the dispute. Within seconds, it appeared different, less urgent, and as though there were less on the line. I found myself feeling less tense, and I even began to see the other person's point of view. As soon as I was able to get away from it, it seemed less personal. It was much easier to deal with and, ultimately, much less difficult to resolve.

I encourage you to try the same thing. The next time you find yourself irritated or sweating the small stuff, see if you can put some distance between yourself and whatever is bugging you. You just might find that the tiniest bit of space is all you need to get over it and move on. From a distance, life seems pretty magical, and far more important than most of the small stuff we tend to worry about.

85

PREVENT LITTLE THINGS
FROM BECOMING
FRONT-PAGE NEWS

When we get too wound up or uptight, it's easy for little things to begin to seem like front-page news in the morning paper. Everything seems bigger and more urgent. Suppose, for example, that your wife says to you, "Honey, I wish you'd pick up your clothes more often." Rather than take it in stride, or see it as an innocent comment stemming from simple frustration, you take it personally and turn it into something much bigger. You'll react and blurt out, "What are you talking about? I picked up my clothes just yesterday. You're always accusing me of things."

As a result of being too uptight, you read things into your wife's comments, think about them too much, and turn them into so much more. You think about how many times she's done this in the past, and how ungrateful she is for all that you do. In the end, this attitude exacerbates the problem and makes you feel frustrated. It certainly does nothing to solve the problem, or to enhance your communication with your partner.

The truth is, even if you thought your wife was being too hard on you, and you felt the need to discuss the issue with her, the best thing you could do, in my opinion, would be to keep your cool and your perspective. By not thinking of it as such a big deal, you're able to determine the best possible response, as well as the best way to deal with it. The same would be true almost regardless of what you were going through—an issue having to do with your kids, a friend, something that happened at work, a dispute with a neighbor.

The act of slowing down from the inside enables us to respond to the events around us, rather than reacting quickly and habitually. Reminding ourselves, again and again, that life isn't an emergency—it only seems that way sometimes—helps us to see things more clearly. Slowing down and taking deep breaths has the effect of allowing us to see things as they really are, instead of as we imagine they are. It takes away that sense of urgency and that need to fight back that so often occurs when we're tense.

Part of the way to lessen the tendency to see things as front-page news is to simply be aware of the disadvantages of doing so. That way, as stuff comes up and you find yourself overreacting, you'll be able to take a step back and remind yourself, "Maybe this is really a smaller article that belongs on page twenty-two."

All news, even front-page news, comes and goes. The advantage of seeing things as smaller rather than larger is that they disappear from your awareness even more quickly. That way, you can spend less time focused on the dramas of daily living and more time having fun and appreciating your life.

86

USE COMPLIMENTS AS A
STRESS-REDUCING TOOL

Almost everyone loves to receive compliments. And why not? Compliments are an acknowledgment of some kind, and they feel good to the spirit.

Aside from the fact that dishing out genuine compliments is a nice thing to do, there are two other very good reasons to offer even more of them in the future. Both of these reasons contribute to a less stressful life.

The first reason you'll want to use compliments freely and often (as long as they are genuine) is because, when you do, it reinforces to the person receiving the compliment that you are a thoughtful person who cares about them—and acknowledges them. As you offer a sincere compliment to your spouse, child, or someone else you love, for example, it gives them a reputation to live up to, in a positive way. It encourages them to shine in your eyes, and it's a way of telling them you appreciate and love them. In turn, they will be inclined to love you even more. The compliment will reinforce your love for them, and remind them of how much they care for you. It's sort of like putting money in your relationship bank. It's one of those hidden treasures of life.

Similarly, when you offer a compliment to someone you work with, or someone you would like to work with, it encourages him or her to see you in a positive light. Since most people don't give very many compliments, it sets you apart. When that person thinks of you, the thoughts he or she has will probably be positive.

When someone is given a compliment, it makes him or her want to like you and want to see you succeed. It's just one more reason—a good one, too—for them to want to be kind to you and to help you. Obviously, when people are kind to you and trust you and love you, your life will be easier.

The other major reason for giving plenty of compliments is that, pure and simple, it feels good to do so. Compliments are the opposite of criticism. If you pay attention to how you feel when you criticize someone, you'll notice that you feel a bit deflated. It can be subtle, but it's usually there. You've just put someone down, corrected them, or made them wrong. And now you and that person get to experience the effect of that negativity.

On the other hand, when you offer compliments, the opposite is true. Not only do you make someone else feel good, but you get to feel good, too. It's an immediate payback. If you pay attention to how you feel when you make someone feel good with a compliment, you'll see what I mean. You will probably notice an immediate shift upward in the way you feel.

I can't think of any downside to giving compliments. It's easy to do, it helps your relationships, makes others feel good, and contributes to your own sense of joy. Giving compliments is a great way to make your life, and the life of others, just a little bit better.

87

KEEP IN MIND THAT PRACTICE
DOESN'T MAKE PERFECT—
PERFECT PRACTICE
MAKES PERFECT

When I was younger, I was a competitive tennis player. I heard a line that changed the way I attempted to practice my game and, I believe, made me a much better player. The words came from the great football coach, Vince Lombardi: "Practice doesn't make perfect—perfect practice makes perfect."

In sports, it's helpful to know this because, otherwise, you could be spending many hours practicing something—but in reality, you might be doing nothing more than practicing bad habits. When this happens, you reinforce problems through your practice instead of correcting them.

I think this idea is even more important in our daily lives. Many of us spend lots of time alone, in our heads. Whether we're in the shower, driving, or taking public transportation; riding in elevators, sitting at our desk, or jogging; we have plenty of opportunity in our lives to be thinking.

The critical question is, What is the predominant theme of your thinking during these and other quiet moments? Are you busy being caught up? Are you planning, solving problems, and anticipating others?

Are you plotting revenge or rehearsing conflicts? Are you sweating the small stuff in the silence of your own thinking? According to what men have been telling me, once they start paying attention, they realize that these are precisely the types of thoughts that fill their minds. I fall into this mental trap frequently. However, it has happened less and less since I've become aware of the problem of "imperfect practice."

If there's one thing we know about men, it's this: We are usually able to get really good at the things we practice the most. Unfortunately, this works both ways. In other words, if we're practicing (perfectly), then the fruits of our practice will be positive. On the other hand, if we're practicing a bad habit, then the end result won't be so good. We'll be getting better and better at something we're not doing so well.

It's easy to see how this works with your tennis game. Imagine that for two hours a day, five days a week, you slapped the ball with a limp wrist while daydreaming about something else. Over time, your backhand would get so bad that you might never hit the ball into the opposite court. On the other hand, if you had some good initial instruction, learned the proper technique, and practiced keeping your eye on the ball, you'd probably get better in no time.

Similarly, if any of us were to spend a great deal of time rehearsing unhappiness (in our own mind) in one form or another, then, over time, we'd become really good at it. Obviously, it wouldn't be intentional, but would rather be an unintended consequence of our mental actions.

If you think about it for a moment, it's pretty obvious. Suppose you're driving and, for an hour and a half, you mentally rehearse a conflict you're sure you're going to experience later that day. Or you're daydreaming and the entire dream is spent trying to resolve your never-ending list of problems and reminding yourself how busy you are. Or imagine that you're on your way home, and you spend the entire time mentally reviewing all the things that are wrong with your marriage.

We all engage in this type of mental activity from time to time, and any isolated set of thoughts probably aren't going to make much of a difference. The problem is when this type of thinking becomes a habit—so much so that we're not even aware that we're doing it. Our thinking patterns become so ingrained that we never stop long enough to question them. We simply go on practicing, practicing, and practicing some more. We don't think of this as practice, but that's really what it amounts to. The question is, What are we practicing? The answer, I believe, is unhappiness.

By becoming aware of our own mental habits and making some subtle shifts, we can change that which we practice into something more productive. Try becoming aware of the types of thoughts you are having—while you're having them. If you find that you're narrowly focused on what's wrong, see if you can bring some balance into the equation and think, at least some of the time, about what's right.

Obviously, what we think about plays a significant role in how we feel and how we live our lives. By becoming aware of that which we practice, we empower ourselves to be happier and more fulfilled. Instead of practicing various forms of negativity, we can transform our practice into a more perfect practice.

88

BE MORE GENEROUS

I'm going to suggest that all of us become more generous—but not only for the obvious reasons you might think. Sure, being generous is an honorable way of being. It takes humility, courage, kindness, self-lessness, and ethics to be a generous person.

The benefits of being more generous, however, extend far beyond the kindness aspects. In fact, being more generous is one of the easiest and most effective ways to become less stressed and uptight. You'll discover that men who are very generous—with their money, time, stuff, ideas, and love—are not very likely to sweat the small stuff. Here's why.

The act of being generous means that you are geared toward giving. You're willing to let go of things—your time, possessions, money, free time, and so forth. To some degree or another, a generous person isn't consumed with protecting his own special interests; at least, it's not an obsession. This lack of holding on to things suggests that he will tend to not be very stubborn. It will be pretty easy for him to let go of things—hassles, imperfections, mistakes, and so forth—the stuff people usually sweat. Generous people often feel as though they have less to lose. This secure feeling tends to make them less defensive individuals who are willing to admit when they are wrong. To them, it's not a big deal to make a mistake, as long as they learn from it.

The very nature of generosity is humility. Therefore, it lends itself to the ability to apologize easily. So, when such a person makes a mistake, it's usually a nonissue shortly thereafter. Instead of defending his actions, denying any responsibility, or blaming it on someone else, he simply admits it's his fault—and moves on. This saves an enormous amount of time and eliminates resentment.

Generous people delight in the success of others and enjoy sharing their gifts and talents. They are willing to share the spotlight—or to step aside entirely when it's someone else's turn. The abundance in their heart is stronger than their need for attention. This makes a generous person easy to love and respect, making his life more joyful and effective.

All of these reasons, and others, contribute to making the life of a generous person much easier than that of someone who is selfish or unable to be giving. A selfish person, who is consumed with his own wants, needs, and desires, is in constant conflict with much of the world. Everything must go his way or he feels threatened or bothered. He often sees people as "out to get him"—or his things—thereby creating a defensive environment. He lives with a great degree of angst and fear, constantly looking over his shoulder.

Generous people, on the other hand, are free from most of these concerns. They feel blessed to have what they have, and even more blessed to be able to share it with others. Without the fear and suspicion associated with a lack of generosity, a generous person is free to experience the joys of life—without sweating the small stuff.

I think it's safe to say that all of us men could stand to be a bit more generous. And since there's no good argument against doing so, and because there are so many quantifiable inner rewards, it's a great way to create a brighter, happier life. It's fun to imagine how the world would change if every single one of us would commit to becoming at least 10 percent more generous right now. While we can't control what others do, or don't do, in this regard, we can make the commitment ourselves. I'll tell you what: I'll do it if you will.

89

LET OTHERS BE RIGHT
ABOUT THE LITTLE THINGS

I'm writing this strategy on a very crowded airplane. When we were boarding the flight, the man sitting next to me claimed that he had the aisle seat. He didn't. He was confused about the seat assignments, but he was determined to be right. I'm a frequent flyer and know the system quite well, and I prefer the aisle whenever possible, because I'm a very tall person.

At any rate, he was quite insistent, and I could see that he was going to make a fuss about it. Rather than turn it into a big deal, prove he was wrong in front of others, and have him mad at me for the next four-and-a-half hours, I simply smiled and said, "You're right, no problem."

Right about now you might be thinking one of two things. "Richard's a really nice guy," or "Boy, is Richard a pushover." And while I'd like to believe I'm a nice person, that really had very little to do with why I gave up my rightful seat (which, by the way, I had booked months in advance). I can also say, without much hesitation, that I'm really not much of a pushover either. When I feel the issue warrants it, I can be as tough as the next person.

The reason I gave up my seat had to do with the fact that in a vast majority of the cases, it's simply not worth sweating it. I say that, not because it sounds good in this particular book, but because it's the absolute truth.

I have found that a vast majority of the time, any satisfaction I receive in convincing myself and/or someone else that I'm right is far outweighed by the effort it takes and the negative feelings it brings to myself and the other person, as well as the conflict that is invariably created.

Think about what would probably have happened if my fellow passenger and I had gotten into a heated debate over the seat selection. (Believe me, I've seen this exact scenario played out on airplanes dozens of times, always with the same result.) We would have made a scene, and both of us would have been upset. Then, only one of us would have been able to get our way, leaving the other upset and angry. The person who secured the seat of his choice would have probably felt a tad guilty sitting there, knowing the other person was furious at him. There would have been tension. And for what? A preferred seat on a few hours' long flight.

It's a great analogy because it's symbolic of any of thousands of similar types of examples. Daily living lends itself to minor disputes or differences in opinion—happens all the time. Who got there first? Whose idea was it anyway? That's my parking spot—no, it's mine!

The less attached we can become to being right, the easier it is to stop sweating the small stuff. Does this mean it's never appropriate to fight for your seat or to prove yourself? No, of course not. Obviously, each circumstance is unique, and there's no hard and fast rule. The point, however, is that the emotional cost of being stubborn, defending and proving yourself, and of having to be right, far exceeds the benefits, in most cases.

Recently, a man told me that he had been very stubborn about being right for his entire life. He had pushed away most of his friends as well as his wife, and most people thought he was a jerk.

Then one day, after reading a book on happiness, he decided to use the magic words. He and his wife were in one of their normal bickering matches when he looked her in the eye and said (sincerely), "I see what you mean, honey. You're right."

That single sentence, simple as it is, opened the door to a major transformation in their marriage. He said he now realized that his wife had probably been waiting their entire marriage to hear those words. That's how powerful they are.

What he discovered was the same thing other men discover when they begin to allow others to be right on little things—it doesn't hurt! We spend years protecting ourselves. We arm ourselves with ego, the opposite of humility. We feel threatened and act defensively. We do this because we want to ensure that we're right on all fronts.

The problem is, other people, especially those closest to us, want to be right, too. And they feel just as certain as we do that they are right. So when one person (you) can rise to the occasion and become slightly more humble, wonderful things begin to happen. Barriers are overcome. Defenses begin to disappear, as do resentments. Communication opens and deepens, and a whole new world begins to unfold.

Believe it or not, it all starts by the simple act of allowing others to be right. The fighting, posturing, proving, and arguing are all lessened. What a great way to create a better life. There are countless opportunities to practice this new way of responding to others. Why not give it a try today?

90

APPLY THE
"ONE-YEAR" STANDARD

In *Don't Sweat the Small Stuff . . . And It's All Small Stuff*, I wrote a strategy encouraging people to ask themselves the question, Will this matter a year from now? I received a great deal of mail from men letting me know that they had never considered this question. Yet, once they did, it tended to put many of their day-to-day small stuff concerns into perspective.

If you can admit that a concern or hassle isn't going to matter even a little bit a year from now, it's often easier to see that it probably doesn't matter very much today. Or, even if it does matter, it might not be worth sweating. There are so many things to deal with in life that if something doesn't meet this standard, we might be better off putting our attention elsewhere, on more important things. It's not that an incompetent employee or a flight delay isn't frustrating to deal with; they are. It's just that in the scheme of things, we're better off letting them go and making peace with the fact that life isn't always exactly as we would prefer it to be. With this more accepting attitude, the minor hassles and disappointments of life are much easier to deal with. We become happier and more effective.

I'm the first to admit that some things will indeed matter a year from now. A death in the family will matter, as will any type of tragedy. If you're seriously injured or ill, it could affect you, not only a year from now, but maybe even for the rest of your life. There are all sorts of serious issues that have little or no relevance to the one-year standard.

On the other hand, a huge percentage of the things that we sweat, probably do apply. Just for fun, I asked a few men to share with me two or three of their top (non–life-or-death) concerns. Here's a summary of some of them: a client or customer was difficult; a dispute with a neighbor; lost keys; traffic and parking problems; criticism; a disagreement or argument with a spouse or girlfriend; a sassy child; a billing error; unreturned phone calls; a computer glitch.

If you were to analyze this list—or any similar list—you'd quickly discover that each and every item on the list would, in all likelihood, be totally and completely irrelevant one year from now. In most cases, in fact, they will probably be nothing more than irrelevant memories within a day or two. In some cases, it might take less than an hour for them to fade into obscurity. So the question becomes, if something is going to most certainly be irrelevant at some point in the not-too-distant future, why sweat it?

Again, there's no need to pretend that things don't bother us. Instead, the idea is to get to the point where they really don't—at least not as much as they used to. By applying the one-year test to the issues that usually bother us, it's easier to move in this general direction.

91

EXTEND COMPASSION TO
YOUR DAILY LIFE

When we see human suffering in person, or even on the evening news, our hearts ache. Many of us are deeply concerned, if not actively involved, with organizations that work on social injustice, hunger, homelessness, and dozens of other worthy causes. My observation has been that, deep down, most men do indeed have compassionate hearts.

It's a bit trickier, however, to act and feel compassionate on a day-to-day, moment-to-moment basis—when you're not witnessing a life-and-death struggle, but a far more mundane incident. With so much less on the line, it's easy to get stuck in our impatience, unrealistically high expectations, and our demanding attitudes.

Luckily, however, there are many ways in which we can become more compassionate in our daily lives. Even little things like becoming less judgmental, making peace with imperfection, allowing someone else to be right, searching for the grain of truth in the opinion of others, and practicing random acts of kindness can make an enormous difference in our own lives and in the lives of others.

I was part of a conversation with a group of men. One man was telling a story and one of his facts was a little off base. I noticed one of his colleagues getting ready to correct him and take center stage. I don't know what it was, but something stopped him. I could tell he was about to say something, but at the last second, he held his tongue.

In the scheme of things, it really wasn't that big a deal. No one was going to die or get hurt if the man had jumped in and corrected his business partner. However, to the man telling the story, it meant a great deal. His story and punch line were well-received with a laugh and a number of smiles. His day, as well as the day of everyone in our group, including mine, was a tiny bit better.

Who knows for sure, but I couldn't help but think that the man who resisted the temptation to correct the speaker knew that he had made a wise choice and felt better as a result. How would he have felt had he ruined his colleague's story when there wasn't any real reason to do so? What would be the point?

When we take the feelings of others into consideration, listen a little more deeply, express gratitude, give someone a break, or engage in a simple act of kindness, we are extending our compassion into our daily lives. If each of us would do this—just a little more each day—then collectively, we'd be making a really big difference.

There is no question that daily compassion contributes to our own happiness. With every gesture of kindness and every patient response, we are the beneficiary of a more peaceful heart.

92

STOP BROADCASTING
YOUR THOUGHTS

You've probably heard the expression "thinking out loud." It refers to the idea that, sometimes, it's helpful (or at least habitual) to be talking about our thoughts as we're having them. It's a way of sorting things out.

There's a fine line, however, between thinking out loud and what I like to call broadcasting your thoughts.

To the best of my knowledge, every one of us, at times, gets mad, frustrated, stressed, anxious, out-of-sorts, grumpy, tired, jealous, and all the rest of it. All of us have fearful, worrisome, angry, or pessimistic thoughts. That's certainly not news to any of us.

The question isn't whether we are going to have negative or self-defeating thoughts stream through our minds—we will. But rather, the question is what do we do with those thoughts when they are right there in the forefront of our thinking?

I've found that it's helpful to know that there are times that we can exacerbate and compound our feelings and problems by broadcasting the negative or insecure thoughts that happen to be in our mind. In other words, rather than seeing our thoughts as thoughts, and keeping them to ourselves, we announce them to others.

Suppose you're in the car with your wife and three kids. You're a bit tired and in a bad mood. At the moment, you're mad at one of your neighbors because she is planning to add on to her home, and you're anticipating a lot of extra noise from the construction.

In this case, there's nothing you can do about the situation. Her permits have been issued, and she's not doing anything immoral or illegal. Furthermore, you've added on to your own house over the years. It's not that big a deal.

But at this moment, you're just in a bad mood and your mind is looking for something to complain about. You're at a fork in the road. You can remind yourself that things always seem worse in a low mood and that you'll get over it. You can decide to keep your thoughts to yourself.

Or you can act on your impulse, which is to bring it up to your family and draw them in. You can broadcast your thoughts to your entire family.

But think about what happens if you broadcast these thoughts in front of your kids. They are going to think you're mad about something you can't do anything about. They probably don't know it's just a mood and that you may not even care about it the next day. In fact, they might imagine all sorts of problems between you and your neighbor. They might worry unnecessarily or even harbor ill feelings toward the neighbor. And while this is a pretty benign example, you have to ask yourself, To what end? What good does it do? And what does it accomplish? The truth is, there might not even be a real issue (other than in this moment) between you and your neighbor—but now your wife and kids think there is.

I'm not suggesting for a moment that there aren't hundreds of times when you will absolutely want to share what's going on in your mind with others. Perhaps most of the time, this will be the case. The trick is to be aware of the difference between sharing because you want to share and because it will be helpful or educational or whatever, versus simply blurting something out because you're having a frustrating series of thoughts.

This strategy can really come in handy and save you a lot of frustration. The next time you're having a thought attack of some kind and are tempted to share with someone else, take a moment to decide if doing so is really in your (and the other person's) best interest. If so, great. Go ahead and share. But if it's not, you might want to bite your tongue and wait for the thoughts to pass. In most cases, that's exactly what they will do!

93

PRACTICE THE RULE OF TWO

Years ago, my friend George Pransky, a wonderful public speaker, shared with me what he called "the rule of three." It had to do with the number of questions an audience might ask during or after a speech. As I understood it, the idea was that if the same essential question came up three times, it was time to start over. In other words, if the audience wasn't hearing the message, it was the speaker who had to alter his or her teaching. It was time to find a new way to explain the material or to come at it differently because it wasn't being explained in a way that it could be heard effectively. The burden was on the speaker, not the audience. Over the years, this idea has helped me to become a better speaker.

What I've found is that a similar idea comes in very handy in day-to-day living, in the area of communication. In other words, there are many instances for all of us when our message simply isn't being heard. We are talking to someone—our child, spouse, someone we work with, even a stranger—and, for whatever reasons, there is a missing link between what we are saying and what is being received. The "rule of two" says that if you've said something twice (or more) and the message isn't getting through, then it might be time to back up—and start over. Maybe it's the way you're saying it or the tone of your voice. Maybe you need to be more philosophic or more specific. Each situation will be different, but whatever you're doing needs to be reevaluated. I changed the number from three to two because, after only two attempts in personal communication, it seems the pattern has already been established.

When we are having a communication breakdown, or we feel we are not being heard, our automatic assumption usually seems to be that it's because of the other person. He or she simply isn't listening. Consciously or unconsciously, we put the burden on them to understand us. It's their fault.

If you step back far enough, however, you can begin to see that, in most instances, this probably isn't the case. After all, if I'm the one who wishes to get across a message, make a request, or deliver some information, wouldn't I be the one responsible for making sure it happens?

I overheard a man screaming on his cell phone to (I'm assuming) his secretary. He yelled out, "I've said this twenty-five times." Even if he was exaggerating, it was clear that he hadn't been able to communicate. But in my book, it's his fault, not his secretary's. He ought to have been less concerned with his secretary's lack of listening, and more concerned with his inability to get across his message in a way that it could be heard.

I've heard many men make the same mistake with their kids (believe me, I have too). We'll say things like, "I've asked you ten times to clean up your room." If we were wise, however, we'd be thinking about our delivery the second time we made the request, instead of repeating ourselves, over and over again, to no avail! Perhaps we need to show our child how to pick up his or her room. Rather than raising our voice and getting frustrated, maybe we need to ask our child to show us (or tell us) how they are going to go about the task.

The same applies to your relationship with your spouse or girlfriend. Perhaps one of your needs isn't being met, or you're frustrated about something. You might think you've been up-front, open, and honest, but it's quite possible that your significant other doesn't have a clue about what's going on. Rather than being mad at her, see if you can make a fresh start. Ask yourself the questions, How can I best get across my thoughts and feelings? and, How can I communicate in a way that she will understand? You might be amazed at how effective this can be.

Imagine you were in a foreign country and you thought you were asking someone for directions to your hotel. In reality, however, your language skills were a bit shaky and you were actually asking them for directions to the beach. Would it be their fault when you ended up at the water? Of course not.

Applying the same logic to your attempts to communicate can greatly reduce the frustration you feel when you're not being heard. Because, rather than hoping that others will understand you, which obviously doesn't always happen, you'll stay more actively involved in the communication process. You'll start to check in with others to be sure you're being heard. And if you're not, you'll simply try it another way.

This isn't to say there won't be plenty of times when you are being clear and the other person simply isn't listening. This is most certainly going to be true some of the time. Nevertheless, in most instances, it's easier to change the way we speak or communicate than it is to hope or insist that someone else will become a better listener. In the long run, this strategy may save you a ton of grief. I'm certain it has done so for me.

94

BECOME A HEALTH NUT

While I'm certainly no expert on health, I do know one thing for sure: When we are as healthy as we can possibly be, we feel better. And while there's no way to quantify it, I'm convinced that the better we feel, the less we are tempted to sweat the small stuff.

When we're fit and healthy, lots of great things can happen. We feel better, of course, but there's more. We look better, feel better about ourselves, sleep better, and have more energy. Women notice, too! No matter what your age, a healthy person exudes energy and, for whatever other reasons, appears sexier than someone who doesn't take care of himself. When you take care of yourself—not superficially, but really make an effort—it shows, and it does make a difference.

When many people talk about health, what they are really talking about is the absence of some noticeable or serious disease. In other words, if you're not sick, you're considered healthy. That's not at all what I'm talking about. When I think of health, it's not just the absence of illness that I'm concerned with, but a genuine sense of vitality. A lack of illness is great, but so much more is possible. Someone who's healthy feels not just okay, but really great. He has plenty of energy to do the things he has to do and wants to do. He is strong and flexible. His body is happy, and so is he. While he can't control everything—for example, his genes and heredity—he does everything within his power to put the odds in his favor.

My parents have always been interested in healthy living. Together they instilled a love of exercise and health in me and in my two sisters. I will always be grateful to them for this gift. In recent years, both my mother and father have become, in my eyes, true experts in health. They appear (and claim they feel) healthier and happier today than they were twenty years ago! I'm not kidding. And they were pretty healthy back then. Both are totally committed to health and fitness. They exercise virtually every day. On a recent trip together, the three of us visited the hotel gym. After thirty minutes of lifting weights, I was ready to call it quits. Both of them, however, continued long after I had returned to my room. Both have become vegetarians and eat only healthy food a vast majority of the time. They read everything they can get their hands on in the areas of health and fitness. They are true inspirations and, if you were to meet either one of them, you would instantly recognize their vibrant health. It shows. It affects they way they feel, as well as their attitude toward life.

It's not impossible, yet it's harder to be upbeat, inspired, calm, patient, and happy when you feel heavy, tired, and stiff (especially if it's self-inflicted). Luckily, we live in a fantastic day and age if you want to be healthy and well-informed on health-related issues. There are so many resources and places to turn. There are great books on diet, yoga, and fitness. Some physicians are experts not only in the treatment of disease, but in fostering optimal health, as well. In fact, tell your doctor that you want to become a vision of health, and ask for his or her advice and direction.

There are great magazines on everything from vegetarian living to lifting weights. One of my current favorite magazines is *Men's Health*. Each month it has great health- and fitness-related information.

I hope I've convinced you to become more proactive about your own health. There are some things you can't change, of course, but there are many ways to enhance the way you look and feel. Obviously, there is work involved, but to me, it's worth every bit of effort put into it.

95

HAVE A FAVORITE CAUSE

In recent years, I've had a lot of fun learning about what brings joy to men. I'd estimate that more than 90 percent of the men I've spoken to who consider themselves very happy (and those who seem the most content to me) have a favorite cause or charity (or several). It's delightful to see grown men glow with pride as they discuss a philanthropic passion. When I question them, all agree that having one has helped them stop sweating the small stuff.

There's no question that having work we love can bring us a great deal of satisfaction. Meaningful work, financial success, and achievements are all important and rewarding. External success, however, fosters a different kind of feeling than does being passionate about a worthwhile cause.

Having a favorite cause or charity can bring tremendous inner satisfaction to your life. It helps you feel connected to the world and as though you're doing something worthwhile for others. When you feel as though you are making a contribution—to whatever cause turns you on—it puts everything else into perspective.

My personal favorite charities tend to work with children, and my personal passion is teaching people to live happier lives. However, I know people who are passionate about everything from world peace to homelessness, and from AIDS research to hospice care. One of my good friends is a committed vegetarian and animal rights advocate. Another finds incredible joy in supporting collegiate debating. Some people are passionate about helping kids, the environment, the elderly, or finding a cure for a particular disease. Some people travel to foreign countries to administer medicine or deliver food to impoverished peoples. Others volunteer at their church or local junior high school. Others strive to save the whales. Still others find joy in teaching people to read or to learn another language. Some people pick up litter on the side of the road. Then there are people who feel that the best way they can be of help is to donate money or to offer their ideas or brainpower. The list of ways to be of help is virtually endless, and in conjunction with everyone else's efforts, it all makes a difference. It makes a difference because it comes from love.

While everyone seems to have their own expression in terms of the way they choose to help, one thing is clear. The involvement in a cause or charity—whatever it happens to be—brings tremendous joy and meaning to a person's life.

It's important to know that having a favorite cause or charity that you help support doesn't have to take a great deal of time. In fact, for most people, it really doesn't. But that's part of the beauty of being involved. It's an incredibly leveraged way to bring joy to your life. The enthusiasm of having a cause you love is enough. Whatever amount of time you spend—and however involved you become—is up to you. But whatever amount you do spend will be worth it.

If you already have a favorite cause, congratulations. Thanks for being a part of the solution and for making the world a better place. If you don't, this is a great time to start. It's easy to become informed about how you can help. Go to the library, surf the web, or simply ask around to find out what others are doing. There's no shortage of great causes and great ways to be of help. Usually, when someone becomes more interested in the area of helping, he or she will be drawn to something specific. Some cause or charity will jump out at you, as if to say, "This one's for you." You'll feel drawn to it. It will touch your heart.

I hope you'll jump on board and get involved, whatever that means to you. You'll be making a positive difference in our world.

96

RESPECT THE LAW
OF DIMINISHING RETURNS

In our "more is better" society, this lesson can be a hard one to embrace. I think this is especially true for men. We're taught, early on and regularly, that whatever we have, it couldn't possibly be enough. Instead, the goal is to get more—money, power, things, friends, experiences, whatever. Without even being aware we are doing so, we apply the "more is better" philosophy to our daily lives. And because of it, I believe we suffer.

Most of us love a great meal, but how many of us know when to stop? Our habit of wanting more instead of enough encourages us to overeat. Many of us do the same thing when we drink. Instead of knowing when to stop, we keep on going. When we work, we do the same thing. Forty hours seems good, so why not more? Then again, why stop at fifty? Wouldn't more be better?

We can always justify more being better, of course. In fact, if you don't buy into the philosophy, you might experience ridicule. I've brought this topic up on numerous talk shows and have been asked many times, "What's the matter, are you against success?" The question is asked in a way that suggests that you couldn't possibly be successful (or even care about success) unless you were a neurotic mess.

Knowing when enough is enough can be a delicate art. After all, having a car is a privilege and a convenience. Wouldn't two be better? How about three? At what point does the privilege become a burden? I don't think there is a specific answer. The key, I believe, is in constantly asking the question of yourself.

Whether it has to do with how much coffee to drink or how much allowance to give to your kids, there's a point at which you cross the line of diminishing returns. In other words, the benefit of adding more is reduced with each added unit until, at some point, it's downright destructive. If you were trying to teach your seven year old about money, a few dollars a week might be okay (or not), but I doubt an argument could be made that $100 per week would be in his or her best interest, even if you could afford it.

Just yesterday I was talking to a man who has eight homes. I asked him if he enjoyed having so many, and he responded by saying, "You must be kidding. It's a pain in the butt." He said he had become "a servant to his servants," long ago. In other words, taking care of his things had become a full-time job.

So here's a man who has clearly "made it," by almost every standard imaginable. Yet, he's too busy taking care of and managing his stuff to enjoy it, even slightly.

Many of us will never own even one home, much less eight. On the other hand, there's a lesson in there for all of us. At what point do we have enough? When do we have enough responsibility, debt, possessions, friends, plans, and everything else?

Again, I don't have any answers regarding this topic—only questions. I encourage you to take a look at your own life and ask the same questions. You might decide that you have enough of whatever it is you're considering. If you do, you might also discover that you can experience more joy with what you do have when you're not longing for more. I'll end this strategy now, because I don't believe more would necessarily be better!

97

BE A QUITTER

Now that I've got your attention, let me explain what I mean. Men are notorious for taking on too much. We pile on more and more responsibilities in our already maxed-out lives. We work long hours, and most of us are attempting to be active, participating husbands and fathers.

But it doesn't stop there. It's hard to say no. So, when asked, we'll sit on a board, mentor another person, volunteer at our church or in the community, coach a soccer team, or help out a colleague. We'll take on new projects—work related, home related, or whatever. We'll help others too, by offering to fix a fence, solve a problem, put together a deal—you name it. There are countless ways we keep adding things to our to-do list. In fact, it's never-ending. And, for the most part, we can easily justify each commitment. We're helping others, contributing, and feeling good about our efforts. But like most things, there's a point of diminishing return.

The first step in becoming less overwhelmed, of course, is to stop making the problem worse. In other words, we must learn to say no by setting limits and boundaries. Beyond that, however, an almost surefire way to begin to reclaim your life is to develop the courage and wisdom to know when and what to quit.

Randy was involved in his child's PTA and volunteered in his class-room. He chaired two committees and sat on two boards. He had a full-time (plus) career and an hour-and-a-half commute each way. He was planning to become his son's basketball coach, as well. I met him at a social function where he told me he attended a number of similar func-tions each month. He seemed to be going crazy.

I can't help but think how much less hectic Randy's life would be if he could muster the courage to quit a few of his ongoing obligations. I say "courage" because it's hard to disappoint others when they're counting on you. But in many cases, it's worth it. I've met numerous men who did, in fact, decide to quit certain activities or optional endeavors, and I've yet to meet anyone who regretted it. The reason is this: Most people realize that when they're operating at their ideal level of commitment, they're effective, helpful, loving, on-target, and having a good time. When you're overcommitted, however, everything begins to fall apart. Things slip through the cracks. You make mistakes, rush around, become less patient, and so forth.

It's hard to realize that often, when you agree to do something, you're not really agreeing to a one-time effort, but instead you're being roped in to an ongoing commitment. I've often done something for an individual or an organization, only to find out later that they were expecting me to do it again—and again and again. It was only by quitting that I was able to free my time to do other things or simply to have more time.

Becoming overwhelmed is a little like becoming overextended finan-cially. It's no one thing that does you in. It may not be the health-club membership, the meals at restaurants, the second car, or the new suit. But all added up, it's too much to handle. So it is with our schedules. Each commitment may only take an hour or two a month, but add it all up and it's pretty awesome. After all, there are only around 720 hours in a month. When you subtract work hours, family time, sleep, and a few special commitments, there's not as much left over as you might think. It's only a matter of time before it simply becomes too much. The only viable solution is to start cutting back.

It's totally up to you what you decide to quit. But when you sit quietly with a pencil and paper to compute the way you spend your time, it usually becomes pretty obvious. There are certain things you can't quit, and other things that are out of the question. That leaves the rest of it.

Although "quit" is indeed a four-letter word, it's often a perfect tonic for an overwhelmed life. And while it can seem, at least initially, that you're giving up something by quitting, in the end you'll probably realize that, in reality, you're gaining more than you're giving up. You're getting back your time and your sanity—and what could be more important than that?

98

REMIND YOURSELF—ONE MORE
TIME—OF THE MOOD FACTOR

I had an experience the other day that was so powerful and helpful, I felt I needed to share it with you. This is one final reminder of the power of moods.

I was in a really negative mood. I was feeling down and overwhelmed (not a great combination). I walked into my office and almost tripped on the stacks of paper surrounding my desk. There were so many unreturned phone calls and requests that they no longer fit on the desk—they were being diverted to other places.

I started to think about how long it was going to take to get through these piles. I had tried, unsuccessfully, the day before, to reach several people. I was working on a deadline, negotiating a new project, and was overextended.

I was feeling sorry for myself, as if I needed some time off. Then it hit me—I was in a really low mood. While I had been in a low mood all along, I didn't know it.

As is often the case with my low moods, I thought the problem was my life—my piles of work and phone calls to return. The deadlines. All the people. The new deal. The expectations. My office space. My overhead.

But I was wrong. And the way I knew I was wrong, beyond any

shadow of a doubt, was that, as soon as I realized that I was in a low mood, I suddenly remembered that what I was facing that morning was essentially the same thing I face many mornings: work-related projects and challenges. I always have an overhead, phone calls to return, and people to talk to—along with all the rest. The difference is that when my mood is good, it doesn't seem like a big deal at all—I simply attend to one thing at a time and do the best I can. It's never totally finished, it's just one thing after another, as I'm sure it is in your life, too. In a higher mood, however, it never seems like a big deal. It's just work, and I usually love it.

The same work and similar hassles, when experienced in a lower mood, suddenly seem overwhelming.

A light went off: If the problem wasn't the work but rather my mood, then what was the big deal? The conclusion I came to was that there wasn't one. My mood would pass—as it always does.

The simple recognition that my low moods affected my outlook and attitude—and that I was currently in one—saved my day. All of a sudden, as soon as I recognized the mood factor, the pressure and sense of being overwhelmed seemed to disappear. After creating some space among the piles, I sat down and got to work.

Looking back, as I reflect on that day, everything went fine. I shudder to think of what kind of day it would have been had I not recognized the mood I was in and how it was affecting me.

I hope you can borrow from my experience and apply it to your own life. I've found that, for me, being aware of my moods is a helpful tip that assists me in keeping my perspective.

99

ASK THE QUESTION,
"IF NOT NOW, WHEN?"

Last summer was a particularly busy time. I had several writing deadlines, as well as a number of important projects I was working on. At the time, my youngest daughter was really into tennis, and some of the world's top women players had come to town to play in a tournament.

A friend was kind enough to offer us two tickets, and my daughter was thrilled. The only problem was, the tickets were for the next day, right in the middle of the work week.

Something happened to me that night as I pondered the pros and cons of taking a day off at that particular time. It was as if a voice inside of me whispered, "If not now, when?"

The question itself was (and is) far more significant than the specific details of this particular instance. It's so tempting to keep postponing and set aside those things we claim are most important. We keep telling ourselves, "Once I get through this, I'll start prioritizing differently." What I realized that night was that, most of the time, we're only fooling ourselves.

Logically, it's easy to see. My daughter is only going to be eight years old for a short period of time. She's home for the summer, out of school, and has plenty of time. She's dying to do something, just the two of us.

She loves tennis. The world's best players are less than an hour away. And we have tickets.

Our decisions, however, aren't always logical. Instead, we create dramas in our minds, build up the importance of our deadlines and other obligations and put off that which, deep down, we know is most important and nourishing about life.

An acquaintance once said to me, "Most men I know spend most of their adult lifetime striving to get ahead—in order to build a swimming pool, for example. By the time they get one, their kids no longer want to use it or spend time with their dads."

Obviously, everyone's situation is different. Not everyone can choose to take a day off in the middle of the week, even if they want to. And I can't always make that decision either. Yet, it's important to remember, if we want a fulfilling life, that time has a way of passing us by. One day flows into the next, which becomes a week, then a month, a year, ten years, and so on. The next thing you know, you're saying, What happened to all that time?

I'm happy to report that we went to the tennis tournament and we had a great time together. More importantly, I was reminded that work will always be there—but my daughter won't be. What I've learned is that the easiest way to avoid regrets is to ask myself the question, "If not now, when?" It's a powerful way to put life and our decisions about how we spend our time into perspective.

100

DEEPEN YOUR PERSPECTIVE

In his most recent book, *Family Wisdom from the Monk Who Sold His Ferrari*, my friend Robin Scharma tells a nail-biting story about his could-have-been-fatal plane crash. Turns out, it's really true—your life does flash before your eyes.

To me, the most interesting part of his story had to do with his description of what happens to one's priorities during moments such as these. Robin said that, in a matter of seconds, you realize that everything that had always seemed so incredibly important in life suddenly seems pretty irrelevant. The size of your bank account, the internal rates of return on your investment portfolio, the lack of hair on your head, the grudges you've held on to, aren't nearly as important as you had imagined they were. Our golf score, business failures, the type of car we drive, items we weren't able to cross off our "to-do" list, fall into the same category—as do most other things.

On the other hand, you suddenly realize that the reverse is also true. The things you may have taken for granted—friends, kids, spouse, freedom, nature, eyesight—suddenly take on a huge significance. The gift of life itself seems magical, to be treasured. The laughter of a child brings a smile to your face. The beauty of nature seems awesome.

This same realization came to Kris and I when our car skidded out of control on a huge sheet of black ice in Wyoming the year before we were married. Our car spun around in circles before being smashed by a huge semitrailer truck. Somehow we ended up in the center section of the freeway, our car crushed. People ran toward us, obviously fearing we were dead.

While we were spinning, as well as afterward, when we were lucky to be alive, our lives looked very different to us. We had, and have maintained to this day, a heightened appreciation for the gift of life. The simple act of walking seemed like a miracle. I remember looking at my mangled car, grateful that it was strong enough to help save our lives— but also completely detached from the fact that my beautiful car had been destroyed. Who the heck cares about a car after something like that happens?

It's interesting, however, how often someone goes completely crazy when the slightest dent or even a scratch shows up on his car. When I see people react this way, I often assume they must have never been in a serious accident. If they had, they might feel differently. Obviously, I'd never wish a bad experience on anyone. I can tell you, however, that most people who come out of a bad accident alive do so with a new sense of joy and a much deeper perspective. Rather than sweating the small stuff—you appreciate it.

The truth is, none of us knows how long we have on this planet. Maybe you have fifty more years—or maybe it's fifty days. Who knows? I certainly don't. But admitting to yourself that you don't know how many years (or days) you have left can be a very liberating experience that can put many things into perspective. It can remind us of what's really important. Every day, I use the fact that I don't know how long I have to live to enhance the quality of my life. I remind myself of what's really important in life, and try to back that up with my actions and the way I prioritize things.

I'd like to end this book with one of the most powerful quotes I've ever seen or heard. It pertains to this notion that life is too precious to take for granted. It has brought enormous perspective to my life, and I hope it does the same for you, as well. I encourage you to read it slowly and to refer to it often. The quote is from Stephen Levine, and it goes like this: "If you had an hour to live and could make just one call, who would it be to—and what would you say—and why are you waiting?"

Treasure yourself and the gift of life.